D1166050

The Secret of Overcoming Verbal Abuse

The Secret of Overcoming Verbal Abuse

Getting Off the Emotional
Roller Coaster and Regaining
Control of Your Life

Albert Ellis, Ph.D.
Marcia Grad Powers

Melvin Powers
WILSHIRE BOOK COMPANY

Published by Wilshire Book Company
9731 Variel Avenue, Chatsworth, California 91311-4315

Library of Congress Catalog Card Number: 99 076880
ISBN: 0-87980-445-9

Printed in the United States of America

IMPORTANT NOTICE: The ideas, procedures, techniques, and suggestions in this book are intended to be for educational and informative purposes and in no way a substitute for professional advice from a duly licensed mental health practitioner or physician, or a deterrent to the timely contacting of appropriate authorities if there is any apprehension as to physical violence. The coauthors and publisher specifically disclaim responsibility for any adverse effects directly or indirectly resulting from the use or application of any information contained in this book.

The case histories, personal experiences, and examples contained in this book are derived from the coauthors' clients, students, and readers. All names and identifying characteristics and circumstances have been changed and may also have been combined for editorial purposes.

To our clients, students, and readers of our previous books who courageously shared their personal stories of verbal abuse, motivating us to write this book.

Our gratitude to our indispensable editor Carole Foley for her heartfelt involvement, her insightful contributions, and her unwavering dedication to the completion of this book.

Our sincere appreciation to our publisher, Melvin Powers, for his continuous enthusiasm during our writing of this book and for his conviction that it will make a major difference in the lives of countless women who deal every day with one of the most disturbing and challenging societal issues of our time.

Contents

PART IV

Getting Past the Fears and Anxieties That Keep You Stuck... No More Staying for the Wrong Reasons or Suffering After You Have Left

PART V

Living Happily Ever After

About the Authors

Albert Ellis, Ph.D., born in Pittsburgh and raised in New York, holds M.A. and Ph.D. degrees in clinical psychology from Columbia University. He has held many important psychological positions, including chief psychologist of the State of New Jersey and adjunct professorships at Rutgers and other universities. He is currently president of the Albert Ellis Institute in New York; has practiced psychotherapy, marriage and family counseling, and sex therapy for over half a century; and continues this practice at the Psychological Clinic of the Institute in New York City. He is the founder of Rational Emotive Behavior Therapy (REBT) and the originator of modern Cognitive Behavior Therapy (CBT).

Dr. Ellis has served as president of the Division of Consulting Psychology of the American Psychological Association and of the Society for the Scientific Study of Sex; and as an officer of several professional societies including the American Association of Marital and Family Therapy, the American Academy of Psychotherapists, and the American Association of Sex Educators, Counselors, and Therapists. He is a diplomate in clinical psychology of the American Board of Professional Psychology and of several other professional boards.

Professional societies that have given Dr. Ellis their highest professional and clinical awards include the American Psychological Association, the American Counseling Association, the Association for the Advancement of Behavior Therapy, and the American Psychopathological Association. He was ranked as one of the "Most Influential Psychotherapists" by both American and Canadian psychologists and counselors. He has served as consulting or associate editor of many scientific journals, and has published over 700 scientific papers and more than 200 audio and videocassettes. He has authored or edited over 65 books and monographs, including a number of bestselling popular and professional volumes.

Marcia Grad Powers holds a degree in education and a California state teaching credential. She has lectured on psychological and personal growth topics to business and professional groups and at numerous colleges and universities, and has been interviewed on a variety of radio and television shows.

As senior editor for 18 years at Wilshire Book Company, which specializes in psychological and self-help books, Ms. Powers has worked extensively with psychologists, psychiatrists, counselors, and other mental health professionals. She has participated in intensive training workshops in REBT for continuing education credit for psychotherapists and has received private instruction in REBT from Dr. Albert Ellis, who considers this book her REBT thesis and who personally accredits her as an REBT educator.

She is the author of three previous books (written under the name Marcia Grad), which have been translated into numerous languages: *A Taste for Life, Charisma: How to get "that special magic,"* and *The Princess Who Believed in Fairy Tales.*

Preface

We have learned much since the 1980s when the first major books explaining the dynamics of abusive relationships became popular. We now know about such things as codependency and dysfunctional families, and have begun to learn how to take care of ourselves emotionally, making our lives better—whether we want to stay, need to stay, or plan to leave our verbally abusive relationships.

Those of us who stay, as many of us do, unfortunately find that *knowing* why things are as they are and *learning* some new ways to make them better doesn't necessarily make us *feel* much better. No matter how much we know about our situation, how much we practice new ways of responding to our abusive partner, and how much better we try to treat ourselves, the daily battle to hold on to our sanity continues. The insecurity, guilt, anxiety, and depression continue too. We struggle valiantly to find some semblance of inner peace and bring some modicum of happiness into our existence. Yet, often inner peace and happiness elude us, even if we leave and life becomes immeasurably better.

Why, if we've learned so much, can't we stop the torment? Why are we still so unhappy? Why do we still get caught up in self-analysis and feel overwhelmed by our own emotions as we attempt to cope with our abuser? Why do most of us stay, hanging on to our cherished happily-ever-after fairy tale, even though it has disintegrated before our eyes? Why do so many of us who leave, return again and again? And why do so many of us who finally leave for good end up in another abusive relationship?

As an author of self-help books, a psychological and personal growth lecturer at colleges and universities, and senior editor at Wilshire Book Company (which specializes in self-help books), I (M.G.P.) have heard these kinds of questions asked time and again by people who are being or have been verbally abused. Such questions have come up repeatedly in letters from readers of my books, in discussions with my students, and in manuscripts submitted by aspiring self-help authors. These people, predominately women, express the pain and emptiness of feeling alone, the frustration of not being understood, the systematic crushing of their self-acceptance and self-love, and the disillusionment and disappointment of having had their fairy tale destroyed. They feel as if they are on a runaway emotional roller coaster with their abuser at the controls. They are drowning in a sea of emotion, calling out for help, searching for a lifeline to save them.

Having once felt overwhelmed myself in a verbally abusive relationship and knowing how much it can help to have even one person understand and throw you a lifeline, I wrote lengthy answers to my readers' letters. And I stayed long after my university lectures were over, laughing, crying, hugging, and sharing personal lessons with the groups of students who clearly couldn't bring themselves to leave with the others. For some, it was the first time they had been able to identify the mistreatment they had been receiving as verbal abuse. Others knew they were being abused, yet had denied it, even to themselves. Few of them realized that what they were experiencing is a painful type of psychological and emotional battery that has been classified as a form of domestic violence by the American Medical Association.

Aware of the immense need, I became determined to find a way to help the millions of other verbally abused people I knew were out there, trapped all alone in their emotional prisons. Being preoccupied with this goal and being a writer, it wasn't surprising that soon a sweet little princess's voice in my head began calling to me and insisting upon my helping her tell her story. So began my book *The Princess Who Believed in Fairy Tales*, an empowering allegory that reveals the pain of abuse, feels the pain, heals the pain, and changes one's perception of it forever. Being able to validate, inspire, guide, and empower others with the hard-learned lessons that transformed my life and the lives of those who have told me their stories is one of the most rewarding aspects of my career.

I have received many heartfelt letters from readers in the United States and throughout the world (*The Princess Who Believed in Fairy Tales* has been translated into numerous languages), thanking me for writing "their" story. Many readers said that they no longer felt alone and that *The Princess* had restored their personal power and set them free emotionally. The book has been hugged against hearts, drenched by tears, and welcomed as a dear friend by a wider audience than I had ever imagined—men, women, and children of all ages from all walks of life.

As I received more letters and talked to more people, it became apparent that something else was also needed—practical, everyday techniques that would help abused people reduce their pain, face their fears, and heal themselves and their lives more quickly and more completely than the usual methods had been able to do.

Given the plethora of books, articles, and radio and television programs about abuse, it was difficult to imagine where these techniques would be found if they hadn't been already. Yet, I believed that somewhere out there in the big world was something powerful that had been missed—a key that would unlock the secret of dealing effectively with verbal abuse. Thus my search began.

In the course of my job as an editor, I worked on many psychological manuscripts and had lengthy discussions about various methods and techniques with psychologists, psychiatrists, counselors, and other mental health professionals from all over the world. Nowhere did I find the techniques that would fill the special needs of the abused people who continued to write me. I wished that magically the secret would somehow fall into my lap, but I didn't count on it, of course. I continued searching.

Then one day a manuscript, *the* manuscript, did in a manner of speaking "fall into my lap." It was assigned to me for editing. It was the new, updated edition of a book Wilshire Book Company publishes that had sold 1.5 million copies in previous editions. This internationally acclaimed classic in the field of psychology,

A Guide to Rational Living, teaches a unique and powerful way for anyone to stop feeling miserable about practically anything.

One of its coauthors is Albert Ellis, Ph.D., founder of Rational, Emotive, Behavior Therapy and originator of modern Cognitive Therapy. He is a world-renowned psychologist and lecturer, and director of the Albert Ellis Institute in New York, which attracts clients and trains psychotherapists from all over the world. (I highly recommend that you read *A Guide to Rational Living* as a follow-up to *The Secret of Overcoming Verbal Abuse.*)

As I read the manuscript, I realized that I had finally found exactly what I had been searching for—the key that would unlock the secret of overcoming verbal abuse. I was amazed that the idea of applying Dr. Ellis's therapeutic methods specifically to verbal abuse had not occurred to me before, since I had been familiar with his time-tested techniques for years.

When I told Dr. Ellis I wanted to write a book that would put his life-changing philosophy and techniques within easy reach of people struggling in verbally abusive relationships, he was enthusiastic. Thus began a collaboration I believe was written in the stars. The result is the book you now hold in your hands, *The Secret of Overcoming Verbal Abuse.* The secret disclosed within its pages is admittedly one of the worst-kept secrets of all time. Millions of people have heard of it and used it successfully to deal with a variety of psychological problems. Yet few are aware of how particularly revolutionary it is when applied to verbal abuse.

The Secret of Overcoming Verbal Abuse offers you an entirely new way of perceiving and dealing with your abuse. It contains solid, time-tested, proven techniques that will wrap themselves around you like a thick, warm, protective blanket, insulating you from the pain of the mistreatment you are receiving or have received in the past. These techniques can help you to

- Stop your doubts and confusion about yourself, your perceptions, and what is or was happening to you
- Establish and maintain your emotional equilibrium and put you in control of your emotions and your behavior—whether you stay or leave
- Restore your dignity, self-respect, self-love, and innate personal power

• Experience the inner peace and happiness you have
wanted, wished for, and in tearful private moments
prayed for…perhaps for years

Dr. Ellis and I have written the book I wish I had had the
first time my "Prince Charming" took aim and pierced my heart
with his words. It could have saved me years of torment, tumult,
and tears. We offer you the awarenesses and tools that can set
you free—free from pain, confusion, and fear, whether you stay
or leave. And they will do it more quickly and more completely
than you ever imagined. These same awarenesses and tools can
help you whether you are a teenager or an adult, a woman or a
man, whether your partner is of the opposite or the same sex.* If
you have children, these awarenesses and tools can help you
become a better role model, which will help reduce the risk of
your children carrying a legacy of abuse into their own adult
relationships.

Now let's begin the journey of enlightenment and empowerment that will dramatically change your life.

Marcia Grad Powers
North Hollywood, CA

---

* The terms *abusive partner* and *abuser,* although usually used in this book to
refer to a man, are meant to apply to any verbally, psychologically, emotionally
abusive partner of either sex, whether it be a boyfriend or girlfriend, significant
other, or husband or wife, living with you or apart from you. The term a*bused
partner,* although usually used in this book to refer to a woman, is meant to
refer to anyone who is in a relationship in which he or she is being verbally
abused.

PART I

Enchanted by the Fairy Tale

Heartbroken by the Reality

Chapter 1

Once Upon a Time

Once upon a time there was a little girl who dreamed of finding her Prince Charming and living happily ever after. I (M.G.P.) was that little girl. Perhaps you were too— along with millions of other women throughout the world.

OUR STORY

Once upon a time we believed that someday we would be swept off our feet by a handsome Prince Charming who would love and cherish us forever. We would then be joyful and feel complete. We would feel as special as a princess—an independent, modern-day princess with opinions, goals, and perhaps a career of her own. We would be appreciated and adored by our prince and lovingly placed on a pedestal—a position of high esteem, dignity, and honor. And, once we found our Prince Charming, maybe it was so...for a time.

Then one day our prince, suddenly becoming less than charming, threw a few wounding words at us. For some of us, the words were so subtle that we doubted they could have meant what we knew they meant. For others of us, the words were so blatant that we could hardly believe we had really heard what we knew we had heard. We were stunned, we were hurt, and we were sad. It just couldn't be. Surely our Prince Charming wouldn't say or do anything to make us feel bad. After all, he was our love, our destiny.

He said that we were imagining the whole thing or that he hadn't meant anything by it. He insisted that surely we must *know* he would never say or do anything to hurt us. When we seemed unsure, he said to stop making such a big deal out of it.

Some of our princes blamed us for everything. Some later said that they were sorry, that they loved us and didn't know why they had talked to us that way. They said that they felt pressured, or that they were upset about something and hadn't meant to take it out on us; that we didn't deserve it. Then they begged our forgiveness and promised it would never happen again. And we believed them.

But it *did* happen again…and then again. Our prince's words hit as hard as a fist and cut to the quick like an invisible dagger. We were knocked off balance. We grabbed on to our pedestal tighter and tighter, our mind spinning around and around, faster and faster. It couldn't be…or could it? We couldn't be sure. Maybe we *were* imagining it, but we didn't think so. Maybe we *were* blowing it all out of proportion, but then why did we feel so awful? Was our prince really that mean? No, he *couldn't* be. Surely there must be a reason for the things he said. We questioned. We analyzed. We objected. We tried to do everything he said he wanted. We tried to resolve the "misunderstandings" logically. We tried to talk to him, appeal to him, and explain how we felt. When none of it did any good, we tried with all our might to put the hurtful incidents out of our mind and pretend that everything was still okay. But underneath, we knew better—and so did our stomach, which began to churn.

Day after day, wounding words took careful aim and pierced our heart. We grabbed on to our pedestal tighter than ever, trying with every fiber of our being to keep from toppling from our perch. But the assaults kept coming, finally sending us crashing to the ground. Time and again, dismayed, we picked ourselves up and climbed back atop our pedestal. After a while, we could no longer muster the strength to pull ourselves back up. But it didn't matter anymore. We no longer believed that we belonged up there anyway.

Life on the ground was sad, empty, lonely, and painful. We stopped trusting our own instincts and believing in our own worth.

We hardly knew who we were anymore. We spent more and more time wondering, worrying, hoping, waiting, trying to figure out, and feeling confused. We analyzed, explained, defended, pleaded, begged, screamed, threatened, and we cried. When none of it worked, we became angry and frustrated, frightened and lost, and we cried some more.

Finally, we believed we were going crazy. We had knots in our stomach so often that we forgot how it felt not to have them. We tread lightly, walked on eggs, waited for the other shoe to drop, and anxiously wondered each day who would show up— the loving Dr. Jekyll we believed our partner *really* was, down deep, or the hateful Mr. Hyde he turned into more and more often. Little by little, so slowly that we hardly noticed it happening, we became sick and tired. Eventually, we became sick and tired of being sick and tired.

There was one thing we were sure of: It wasn't supposed to be like this. We felt compelled to determine what had gone wrong—what we had been saying or doing, or not saying or not doing, that kept turning our Prince Charming into a hurtful adversary. We tried to figure out when we had become the enemy, and why we lost battle after battle in a war we didn't want to wage, didn't understand, couldn't believe was being fought—and worst of all—felt completely helpless to stop. There we sat, all alone, surrounded by chaos, with no idea where to turn for shelter or solace, remembering what it used to be like—and sometimes still was—and we hoped and waited and even prayed for things to get better.

After a while a numbing fog settled in and made everything more obscure than ever. Still, we trudged through it, searching for the answers that would set us free from the pain, confusion, and fear. We wracked our brains for a solution, our life seeming to depend upon our finding a way to fix it—but how? Trying to figure it all out became our daily occupation, then our minute-to-minute *pre*occupation.

Why couldn't our prince understand our pain? Didn't he know how much we loved him? Didn't he realize he was our Prince Charming, the man we had dreamed of and waited for all our life? The man we had counted on to make our fairy tale of happily

ever after come true? Why could we handle everything at work
but couldn't handle this at home? And why could we get along
with everyone else in our life but not with the person who
mattered to us most? Didn't anything make sense anymore?

We kept trying desperately to fathom the unfathomable and
fix the unfixable, until finally some of us gave up—but it didn't
make any difference. Either way, we were left alone, trembling
in the dark, wondering if we were losing our mind. Wondering
what ever happened to our best friend—the wonderful Prince
Charming who used to take us in his arms and make the whole
world just drift away. Wondering if we would ever feel that way
again. And wondering where along the way we had lost ourself.
We felt wounded. We felt doomed. Our life and heart were full
of misery and confusion, emptiness and despair. We could see no
way out. We had only questions with no answers, problems with
no solutions, and we couldn't talk about it to anyone—not even
our best friend.

Does the story you have just read sound like *your* story? If
so, some of the following feelings and experiences may describe
your feelings and experiences:

- You get that "certain feeling" that something isn't right,
  but you don't know what it is.
- You feel as if you have been put down, but you can't
  put your finger on the cause.
- Your partner switches from charm to anger without
  warning, often catching you off guard.
- He sometimes treats you as if you were his enemy. He
  frequently gets angry about the most insignificant
  things. What seem like small issues often become big
  battles.
- You feel as if you are walking on eggs most of the time,
  trying not to "set him off."
- You feel upset, tense, drained, angry, sad or depressed,
  and out of control much of the time.
- What angers your partner one day is different from what
  angers him the next. As fast as you fix one thing he
  objects to, he begins criticizing, complaining, or raging

about something else. It seems you can't do enough to satisfy him.

- He expects you to know what he is thinking and feeling, to anticipate his unspoken needs and desires, and to put them ahead of your own.

- You feel as if you are in a no-win situation. No matter what you say or do, or don't say or don't do, your partner twists it around so that you seem to be in the wrong.

- You feel frustrated because your intentions and comments are misunderstood. You find it difficult to have a logical conversation or to resolve "differences." Your partner takes much of what you say as a personal attack or criticism, no matter how unthreateningly you phrase it. At times you feel resentful.

- You rationalize your partner's poor behavior and make excuses for it. You even lie to cover it up.

- You analyze conversations after they take place, trying to figure out what really happened, how you could have handled them differently, and whether you were at least partly to blame.

- Conversations and intentions that at first seem clear become muddled. You feel confused and doubt your view of things. Sometimes you fear you are going crazy.

- Your partner brings out the worst in you, causing you to say and do things you dislike yourself for, yet can't seem to stop.

- You often feel inadequate, incapable, stupid, and bad about yourself.

- If you have children, you feel torn between your relationship with your partner and protecting your children from him. His treatment of you in front of them undermines your authority and control.

- He is possessive and jealous of time you spend with your children, other family members, or friends. He resents the time you spend at your job or at activities in which he is not included.

- He tries to control what you wear and to whom you talk.

- You feel restricted, watched over, scrutinized, and accused of things you did not do.
- Your partner belittles you or calls you names.
- He is mean to you, then later wants sex and blames you for not being in the mood.
- He becomes so angry at times that he throws or breaks things.
- No matter how much you give, how much affection you display, or what loving words you say, you cannot convince him that you love him as much as he loves you. His need for love and reassurance is insatiable.
- When your partner acts nice, you tend to forget his past hurtful behavior and think that he has changed and that things will get better. You think that maybe the good times outweigh the bad.
- You often feel lonely, even when your partner is right beside you. You miss the *him* you used to know and love.
- You cannot tell anyone what you are going through. You don't think you could explain what is going on in a way that anyone else could understand. And you fear you would appear to be the "bad guy" because other people see your partner as a charming, wonderful, likable person.
- You feel trapped and hopeless.

If this chapter has described your experiences and feelings, you are in a verbally abusive relationship. But don't despair; your story is far from over. You can still live happily ever after—though probably not in the way you once thought. This may not be easy for you to believe right now, but you will soon discover how each of us writes our own story and can create the ending we want. It is a matter of learning how. So travel along with Dr. Ellis and me as we lovingly guide you down a new path to emotional freedom.

Chapter 2

Learning the Truth
Your First Step to Emotional Freedom

How many times have you spent the day with your partner knowing that something was wrong, but couldn't figure out what it was? How many times have you begun to shake and had no idea why? How many times has a conversation with your partner started out seeming normal and logical, only to become more absurd, more confusing, and more upsetting as it continued? How many times has your partner erupted into a monologue that grew longer, louder, angrier, and crazier by the minute? And how many times has he "done his damage," and then shut you out to shut you up?

When these kinds of incidents occur, you are likely so caught up in trying to figure out what is going on, dodging verbal attacks, and dealing with your feelings that you can't see the big picture. It is easier to look at these situations when you are not in the middle of them. As you read the following examples of typical incidents that upset abused partners, decide what you think each is about and write down your answer on a piece of paper. Later we will give you *our* interpretations, which may surprise you.

Incident #1

You hang up the telephone after a brief conversation. Your partner says, "So, who were you talking to this time, Mary again—or your *mother*? You spend too much time talking to both of them. They're a bad influence on you. You have no mind of your own."

Incident #2

You tell your partner about an incident at the market in which another shopper was nasty to you. You know you were not the cause of her anger. Your partner says, "Well, you must have done *something* to tick her off or she wouldn't have said that."

Incident #3

You receive a long-awaited promotion at work. Excited, you can't wait to tell your partner. When you do, he says, "Hey, a promotion. That's great!" Then he is quiet and sullen for a week.

Incident #4

You and your partner are leaving for his business Christmas party. He says, "It's probably better if you don't say too much tonight. That way you'll be just fine." He slips his arm around you and gazes into your eyes. "You know I'm saying this for your own good, don't you?"

Incident #5

You and your partner attend a social gathering. You spend time talking to a man who teaches music, one of your longtime passions. The conversation is very interesting. You are animated and thoroughly enjoy it.

Later, your partner gives you a hard time about talking to another man, saying you never seem that excited when you are talking to *him*. He accuses you of flirting and says you always ignore him when you are with other people. Then he launches into a tirade about other times you "slighted" him at gatherings in favor of your friends or family.

Incident #6

You and your partner are about to leave the doctor's office. When you present your parking ticket at the reception desk, you are told the office no longer validates. As you leave the building, your partner says, "They've really gotten cheap." You reply, "It seems that way." He sarcastically responds, "*Seems* that way? It doesn't just *seem* that way; it *is* that way." You answer, "I just meant maybe they had to lower their expenses." He replies, "That's what I just said. Don't you get it? With profits down and malpractice up, they had to cut someplace, so they got cheap with the parking. But you don't know about those things."

Incident #7

You and your partner are driving to a restaurant you have been to only once. Your partner begins to turn left at a certain street. You tell him that you think you are supposed to turn right. He says, "You're wrong! You don't know where you're going! *I'm* the one with the good sense of direction." He turns left.

Your partner drives on for several minutes, then realizes he has made a wrong turn. He starts muttering. You say that it is no big deal and that you only happened to remember which way to turn because of the flower shop on the corner. You suggest he simply turn around and go back to the corner where he should have turned right.

He angrily replies, "Stop telling me what to do! It's your fault we turned the wrong way in the first place. You were yakking so much, as usual, I couldn't concentrate on where I was going."

You start to object but he interrupts, "Just drop it!" He screeches through a U-turn in the middle of the block, barely missing a parked car, then races down the street. You feel trapped. As calmly as you can, you ask him to please take it easy.

Your partner explodes, "I *am* taking it easy! You always think I'm upset when I'm not. You're the one who always overreacts. I wasn't even close to that parked car. If you don't like the way I drive, get out!" Then he turns the radio way up and ignores you.

Incident #8

Your partner usually picks up his clothing from the cleaners. One morning, as you are both leaving for work, he tells you he wants his blue suit for an important business meeting the next day and it won't be ready until after noon. He asks you to pick it up from the cleaners. You reply that you have a late afternoon meeting and don't know if you can get to the cleaners before they close. As he drives off, he hollers, "Make time to do something for me for a change. If you had an appointment to get your hair cut after work, you'd find a way to get there."

You go to work and worry all day about getting to the cleaners on time. Your meeting drags on and on. Your boss is there and you can't leave.

You reach the cleaners just after they have closed and return home without the suit. Your partner angrily says, "I can't count on you for anything! You're never there for me. I only asked one thing of you and you couldn't even do that." You say, "I wanted to get it for you. I tried. I'm really sorry. I couldn't get out of my meeting. I was afraid this might happen."

He replies, "You always have an excuse, but your excuse won't get you out of this. Why don't you just admit it? You didn't try that hard to get there. You only care about yourself! I'm always your last priority." You answer, "No, you aren't. You know how important you are to me. I always put you first. You know that. Why just yesterday I—"

He breaks in, "If you had put me first, I'd have my suit right now!" Then he picks up the newspaper and begins reading it as if you weren't even there.

Incident #9

You have planned a special day for just the two of you. As you are leaving the house, your partner starts to complain about something you did the week before. You get "that old familiar feeling" and know that it's happening again. He is going to somehow manage to ruin the entire day.

Incident #10

You and your partner attend a party where there is considerable drinking. After having a few drinks, he begins dancing suggestively with another woman. When he heads for the bar, you follow him and ask him not to dance with her anymore. You say that people were staring and it was embarrassing. He replies, "I'm just having some fun. Don't make a federal case out if it. If you don't like it, leave." You're so upset that you have a friend drive you home.

Later, your partner shows up in a rage, wakes you up, and yells at you for making a scene and leaving. You explain how upset and hurt you were by his behavior, and you remind him that he told you to leave if you didn't like what was going on. He cuts you off, saying, "I'm fed up with your lame excuses. I never told you to leave. You always claim to remember things that never happened. I wasn't doing anything wrong, no one was staring, and you *always* exaggerate things."

Then he wants to have sex. When you refuse, telling him that you are still too upset, he replies, "Oh, great! The usual excuse. Never mind. Don't do me any favors. You don't turn me on anymore, anyway."

Incident #11

Your partner decides to replace a broken roof-mounted light fixture. He tells you to hold the ladder and hand him the tools as he needs them. You dread what's coming, but you agree, hoping it won't be as bad as usual. You know better than to talk to him. You hold the ladder as steady as you can and hand him the tools as soon as he asks for them. And you don't answer when he yells at you for not knowing which tool he is going to need next.

He asks for a screwdriver. You hand one up to him. He says, "No, no, not the Phillips, you idiot!" While you are reaching for the other screwdriver, he yells, "Hold the damn ladder. It's shaking!" Then he scrapes his hand and says, "Now see what you made me do!" He mumbles some choice words.

The more he mumbles, the more he winds himself up; the more he winds himself up, the more frustrated he becomes, and the more mistakes he makes. He drops one of the screws. "Damn! Get me that screw." You nervously look around for the screw while holding the ladder. "I don't know where it is. I can't see it," you reply. He fires back, "How come you didn't see where it went? You were standing right there!" Then he growls, "These jobs are always twice as hard when you're helping me."

What you *think* these incidents are about is probably not what they are *really* about. And what you think the abusive incidents you routinely experience in your relationship are about is probably not what *they* are really about, either. If you are in a verbally abusive relationship, your view of yourself, of what your relationship is, and of what your Prince Charming is really like are repeatedly being challenged. The way to end your confusion and begin sorting out the reasons for your pain is to learn the truth about what is *really* going on. To do this, you must let go of your fairy tale long enough to see your relationship for what it actually is and to learn some basic facts regarding it.

The more you learn about the dynamics of verbally abusive relationships, the more likely you will realize that much of what you believed about the way your relationship functions is not true, and that much of what you believed about your Prince Charming is not true either. His view of your relationship, his expectations of it, his goals, and the motivation for his behavior are quite different from what you think they are—and quite different from your own. Realizing this is your first step to freedom from pain, confusion, and fear.

WHAT IS *REALLY* HAPPENING WHEN YOU ARE BEING VERBALLY ABUSED?

The incidents you just read about are not what they appear to be. They are not about parking validations or getting to the cleaners on time or the right way to get to a restaurant. They are not about flirting or paying too little attention to one's partner at a social gathering. They are not misunderstandings. They are not ordinary conflicts. They are not about who did or didn't *say* what. They are not about who did or didn't *do* what. They have little or nothing to do with the issues raised. What these incidents are about is one partner's attempt to control the other. Establishing and maintaining this control is the abusive partner's real goal, although he probably is not consciously aware of it. He does this by sending messages that say: "I'm okay," "You're not okay," and "You can't make it without me."

Like the abusive partners portrayed in the incidents above, your partner doesn't raise issues to resolve them, to give you "helpful" advice "for your own good," or to accomplish any other positive goal. His hurtful statements and behavior help him fill his need to feel powerful and to establish control over you. Your focusing on the individual issues causes you to miss the obvious: The issues are *not* the problem. Verbal abuse is the problem. The control he attempts to establish is the problem. The irrationality of what is happening is the problem. The entire interactive process that takes place between you and your partner again and again is the problem.

During this interactive process, you and your partner, cast in specific roles, repeatedly play out similar scenarios. He says or does something hurtful that prompts a reaction from you. Your reaction is a stimulus for a response in him, and so on. Or, you may do or say something innocuous that prompts a hurtful response from him. His response serves as a stimulus for a defensive response from you, which may serve as a stimulus for another attack from him.

Once you are aware of what is happening, you can usually identify familiar themes. For example: He attacks; you defend. He blames; you explain. You cry; he walks out. You try to talk about something that is bothering you; he changes the subject and picks on you about something else; you end up defending yourself about the new issue. In one form or another, you do the same verbal, psychological, behavioral "dance" with each other time after time, unaware of the underlying current that drives these behaviors.

Your partner speaks with authority and confidence, thinking he is absolutely right. He is so convincing that you may believe what he says is true and that he does, as he claims, have your best interest at heart. He may use any combination of abusive behaviors, such as demanding, intimidating, blaming, criticizing, demeaning, ignoring you, or denying that he is doing anything wrong. His behavior is irrational and unpredictable, tends to escalate in intensity, and is characterized by confusing mental games and psychological manipulations. Your abuser may be domineering or quietly controlling. He may be irritable and angry most of the time, or seldom. He may be outgoing or introspective. He may be athletic or intellectual, or both. Every abuser is different and has his own "style" of abusing. But abuse is abuse. To protect yourself from it, you must learn to recognize it in its various forms.

If your partner blatantly uses hurtful words and behaviors, you are probably aware you are being attacked. He may, for example, call you names and accuse you of things you didn't do. However, if your partner's verbal attacks are perpetrated quietly and subtly, you may have difficulty identifying them as abusive. The attacks may not appear to be earth-shattering events, but because they happen repeatedly and are insidious, elusive, and irrational, they can have psyche-shattering results.

Although a fine line exists between subtle and blatant abuse, we will separate them for purposes of discussion. Most abused partners experience both, since the intensity of abuse fluctuates and abusers use different tactics at different times.

Subtle Abuse

Subtle abuse gives you an uncomfortable, unsettling feeling that something is very wrong, but you can't quite figure out what it is. You may get a sick feeling in your stomach, tightness in your throat, or some other physical reaction. When you live with subtle abuse, you become so conditioned to it that it doesn't seem as bad as it once did. Quiet anxiety becomes your new norm. But the cumulative effect over time of multiple instances of subtle abuse can be devastating. Although the variations of subtle abuse are many, they all involve your being treated with disrespect. Here are some of the most common forms you may be experiencing:

- Disapproving, accusatory facial expressions, such as an exasperated or angry face, which your partner denies, implying that you are seeing things.
- Disapproving, accusatory, or sarcastic tones of voice, which your partner denies, usually claiming that you heard it wrong.
- Hurtful remarks delivered in a sincere, caring voice.
- Criticisms of your appearance, the things you say, or the way you say them, which your partner tells you are for your own good.
- Inferences that you are wrong, stupid, careless, inept, or otherwise lacking or inadequate, which your partner denies having meant or said at all.
- Judgments about or denial of the validity of your thoughts, perceptions, or feelings. Your partner insists that he knows your intentions, thoughts, or feelings better than you do. He says that he knows you better than you know yourself.
- Challenges to or condescending remarks about your opinions, beliefs, choices, decisions, goals, dreams, or accomplishments. Your partner often asks for proof before believing what you say.
- Insults, derogatory inferences, or sarcastic remarks, which may include comebacks or put-downs about you,

your family or friends, your job, or the things you like to do. Your partner tells you that he doesn't mean anything by it, he doesn't mean what you think he means, he is only kidding, you are imagining it, or he may deny having made the comment at all.

- Jokes that diminish you, which your partner says you take the wrong way. He accuses you of being too sensitive and of overreacting.
- Repeated remarks that someone else *always*—or *never*—does this or that, implying that the other person is better than you are. When you achieve something special, your partner doesn't see it as any big deal.
- Insensitive or hurtful behavior when you are particularly vulnerable and in need of your partner's understanding and support.
- Insensitive or hurtful behavior that spoils your mood when you are happy or excited about something or are celebrating a special occasion.
- Interruptions by your partner when you are talking. He talks over you, takes over your conversations with other people, or answers questions addressed to you.
- Repeated accusations that you pay more attention to your children, other family members, or friends than to him.

Your partner is also subjecting you to subtle abuse if he does any of the following:

- Twists your words, distorting the meaning of what you say.
- Says what he has to say, then refuses to hear what you have to say.
- Ignores you or will not give you an answer when you ask a question.
- Gives you the silent treatment and denies that anything is going on.
- Keeps his thoughts and feelings hidden from you.
- Often does not show up for events that are important to you, shows up late, or does not dress appropriately.

- Expects or wants you to be home waiting for him even when he doesn't know or doesn't tell you when he will be there.
- Breaks his promises and commitments to you: agrees to do things but doesn't, then claims he "forgot" or tells you to stop nagging him about it.
- Habitually refuses to fulfill small requests that other people would consider reasonable: He won't stop to let you run a quick errand (pick up clothes at the cleaners, for example), when you are driving right by. You are either afraid to ask him to go out of his way to do anything for you, or you do not think it is worth the hassle of asking.
- Routinely puts his wants and "needs" ahead of yours. He insists upon going where he wants to go and doing what he wants to do, and he expects you to go with him without complaining—even if you intensely dislike the activity and do not want to go. When he finally goes where you want to go, he somehow makes you sorry you ever asked him.

Here are examples of some types of power-stealing abusive remarks you may be hearing:

Crazy-making Remarks

"I don't understand. What did I say (do)?" "I didn't say (do) anything wrong." "You know I didn't mean anything by it." "How can you say (think) that?" "You know I would never say (do) anything to hurt you." "I'm telling you this for your own good." "I don't know what you're talking about." "I never said (did) that." "That never happened." "You're just imagining it."

Conversation-stopping Remarks

"That's stupid." "Forget it." "I've heard enough." "Just shut up. It's over." "Who asked you?" "I'm tired of your complaining." "I've had it with you." "You're always overreacting." "Quit making a big deal out of everything." "There's nothing to talk about."

Put-down Remarks

"I told you so." "That's *your* opinion." "You don't have the slightest idea what you're talking about." "Only *you* could do that."

"You're just sensitive." "You're not as smart as you think you are." "Don't talk when you have nothing to say." "I can't believe you would do that!" "Who appointed you ruler of the universe?"

Blatant Abuse

Even when hurtful behavior is blatant and you know you are being attacked, you may not think of it as abusive. It may seem as if you and your partner simply fight a lot, or you may tell yourself that "that's just the way he is," or that because of the stress he is under he has good reason for behaving as he does. Blatant abuse includes such behaviors as:

- Being hypersensitive to everyday occurrences and blaming you for his irritability, anger, or for things that happen to him when you had nothing to do with them.
- Humiliating you in private or in public. Talking to you like a misbehaving child: "Can't you ever do anything right?" "How many times do I have to tell you the same thing?" "Where are you going? I'm not through with you yet!"
- Shouting at you, calling you names, threatening to leave you, or telling you to get out.
- Using criticisms and blaming statements, such as: "I'm sick of your analyzing (or talking) everything to death." "I'm sick of your excuses." "I'm sick of the sound of your voice." "It's your fault. You brought it on yourself." "If it hadn't been for your stupidity, this never would have happened."
- Criticizing you in front of your children or taking their side in a dispute, thereby undermining your parental authority.
- Accusing you of flirting with other men or of having affairs when you are not. Insisting that you dress in a non-provocative way.
- Refusing to go out with you; to socialize with your friends, family, or colleagues; or to allow them to come to your home. Harassing you about seeing or calling them, or being jealous of your time with them. Isolating you from supportive people in your life.

- Refusing to share money or allow you to participate in making decisions involving money.
- Taking away money you earn, your credit cards, or your car keys.
- Forbidding you to leave the house or locking you out.
- Refusing to allow you to work or attend school in preparation for work.
- Insisting on participating in your personal decisions.
- Keeping you up or waking you up to verbally abuse you. Going to sleep or pretending to sleep to avoid hearing what you have to say.
- Trying to have sex with you when you are sleeping or demanding sex when you are tired or ill. Expecting you to have sex with him soon after he has been abusive to you. Becoming angry and blaming when you are still too upset and hurt to comply.
- Confiscating or destroying personal papers, photos, or other items you need or treasure.
- Breaking, striking, punching, or throwing objects. Wielding weapons in a threatening way.
- Threatening to abuse pets to hurt you, or actually abusing them.
- Threatening to harm you or your family.

Some abused women deny the true nature of their relationship and discount the severity of their abuse. Until you are ready to recognize what is going on in your relationship, you will compare your partner's behavior to other people's whose behavior is worse, and say: "My partner isn't *that* abusive. He doesn't do any of *those* things." "Lots of other men are *much* worse." "My situation isn't *that* bad. I can stand it." This is particularly true if your abuse is subtle. But even if your abuse is blatant, you may point to the behavior of physically violent abusive partners you have heard or read about, and say the same things.

Don't fall into this trap of discounting your pain. Until you understand and accept the truth about your relationship, you will be unable to handle it effectively.

Now we are going to talk about the most common pattern of abusive behavior. It's a pattern you will recognize immediately.

THE DR. JEKYLL & MR. HYDE SYNDROME

At the beginning of your relationship, your partner may have been his "nice self" all the time. After a while—typically when he became secure enough in your relationship to know you wouldn't easily walk away—he would sometimes let himself go and behave hurtfully. This does not mean that he consciously planned to do so or that he was aware he had an agenda. Often abuse is a subconscious process. Nonetheless, he "tested" you to see how much he could get away with, just as a small child tests parental limits. If you repeatedly gave in and deferred to him—with or without voicing hollow objections—he learned that he could get away with treating you almost any way he wished.

Abuse usually begins with occasional brief episodes. As time goes by, they become more frequent and last longer. As the balance of power gradually swings in your partner's direction, you increasingly find yourself dealing with a mean stranger instead of the man you knew and loved.

Like most abusers, your partner has probably developed a sixth sense that tells him when he has pushed you to your tolerance limit. Each time you reach that point, he seems to instinctively pull back. He may be the type who stops abusing for a while but never apologizes for his behavior. Or he may be the type who does something nice to disarm you and convince you that your reactions to the abuse are exaggerated. He may bring you flowers, take you somewhere special, or repair something for you around the house. He apologizes profusely and says it will never happen again. Then he treats you better for a while. You let down your guard and once again become vulnerable. Inevitably that is when he resumes abusing you.

Your partner's pattern of unpredictable, dramatic, seesaw personality changes from loving to hurtful and back again become a way of life that grows continuously worse as the number of painful incidents increase and the "loving" times decrease. This cycle is so common in abusive relationships that the phases have been given such names as the honeymoon period, abusive period, and reconciliation period. And abused partners refer to their abuser sometimes as a loving Dr. Jekyll; other times, as a hateful Mr. Hyde.

When your partner is in his Mr. Hyde phase, you hope and wait for the return of Dr. Jekyll. When he is in his Dr. Jekyll phase, you live anxiously in dread of the facial expressions, body posture, or voice intonation that signal he is switching again. Eventually, the Dr. Jekyll periods dwindle, leaving you to deal with a Mr. Hyde most or all of the time. But even if his loving self disappears altogether, you may believe that the man you loved is still "in there" somewhere, and hope with all your heart that one day he will come back to you.

BUT HE'S SO CHARMING

Many abusive partners seem to be charming, passionate people who, during their loving Dr. Jekyll phases, can make your heart palpitate and your knees grow weak. These times can be so wonderful you feel as if you are walking on air. You are reminded of how lovable your partner can be, and how sweet, thoughtful, romantic, and fun he once was. You remember why you fell in love with him in the first place. Your recollections of his abusive periods grow hazy. You become hopeful, again and again, that perhaps things are getting better.

In all the confusion, you may mistake his manipulation for charm and your dependence for love. Here are a few important facts about the considerable charm of many abusers:

- Charm is a skill they acquire—although usually not consciously—to make themselves acceptable, admired, and above reproach (how could he *possibly* be guilty of such horrendous behavior when he's such a terrific guy?).
- Although their charm is highly developed, it is only superficial.
- Being charming is one of the ways they take the offensive to fend off disapproval.
- Knowingly or unknowingly, they use charm as a tool to disguise their true feelings of anger.
- Many people are taken in by the charm of abusers, which makes them effective at disarming, confusing, and controlling their partners.

In this chapter you have begun to learn the truth about what is really going on in your relationship. It is not surprising that what you have been experiencing has had a major impact on how you feel, think, and behave. That is what we are going to talk about next.

Chapter 3

How You Are Affected
What You Think, Feel, and Do

Your first experience with verbal abuse probably shocked, hurt, and confused you. You couldn't believe it was really happening. But after the incident was over, its impact probably faded and you were certain that it would not happen again. Unfortunately, that wasn't the case. The next occurrence shocked, hurt, and confused you again. As the abuse continued, you became less shocked and more hurt and confused—and sad.

Now, long after your abusive partner has caused an incident and left, you continue to suffer. You review the incident repeatedly in your mind, trying to figure out what happened, what your part in it may have been, what you *could* have or *should* have said that might have made a difference. When something else requires your attention, you may momentarily "forget" the incident. But soon your mind returns to analyzing and your body returns to the anxious state you have come to know so well. After a while you may feel the physical signs of anxiety all the time and forget what it was like *not* to feel them.

Any number of thoughts can bring back the mental preoccupation or intensify it, such as thoughts about going home and finding your partner there, or about having him come home to you. Thoughts about when he will revert next to his abusive Mr. Hyde persona; or about what you should have said or done during the last "incident"; or about how to get through to him; or about how he regularly apologizes and says he didn't mean what he said, that you didn't deserve it, and that it won't ever happen again (you know from experience that it will, yet each time you hope it will be different); or about how he denies or brushes off as nothing the hurtful things he says and does; or about how wonderful he makes you feel when he is being his "nice self," the charming self that you "just know" is the *real* him. How many times have you drained your energy with thoughts like these?

EMOTIONAL EFFECTS

As you have endured hurtful words and behavior with increasing frequency and intensity, your suffering has probably grown deeper. You may feel like a failure in your relationship and may have begun to dislike yourself more and more. You may also feel any or all of the following:

- Anxious, tense, fearful, overwhelmed
- Confused, disconnected, disoriented, off balance, out of control
- Frustrated, impatient, angry, resentful
- Lonely, isolated, empty, helpless, hopeless
- Fragile, hypersensitive, depressed
- Inadequate, incompetent, insecure, guilty, ashamed
- Victimized, trapped, depleted

These chronic feelings can take a heavy toll on your mind and body, making you vulnerable to a wide range of mental and physical problems. The stronger you feel these emotions and the longer they persist, the more likely your mind and body will finally break down in some way.

MENTAL AND BEHAVIORAL EFFECTS

You may have experienced some of the following changes in your mental state and ability to function in your daily life:

- You feel distracted, preoccupied, and have trouble concentrating.
- Your ability to perceive, think, and reason is impaired.
- You don't trust your intuition, judgment, or perceptions as much as you used to. You have difficulty making decisions.

- You are compulsive and have obsessive thoughts about your situation.
- You forget things, misplace objects, or are clumsy and accident-prone.
- You sleep too much, work too hard, or keep too busy trying to escape your thoughts and feelings.
- You feel sexually turned off by your partner.
- You have an affair or develop an addiction (such as food, alcohol, drugs, sex, gambling, shopping).
- You sometimes take tranquilizers or mood elevating drugs.
- You are sometimes ineffective at school or work.
- You have difficulty handling your children.
- You become a stranger to yourself, a stranger you don't like. You are impatient and critical, rude and abrasive. You yell at your children and cut off slow drivers. You blow up when you bump your elbow or break a nail. And a glass of spilled milk reduces you to tears or sets off a screaming frenzy. You say and do things you can't believe you have said and done. You may even find yourself becoming downright abusive—if not to your partner, then to your children and others. And you probably hate yourself for it.

PHYSICAL EFFECTS

A prolonged state of emotional stress—especially if you feel out of control, overwhelmed, and helpless—literally undermines and breaks down your tissues and body systems. If you are in the chronic emotional upheaval typical of abused partners, you are at risk of developing a variety of physical problems. These can include everything from annoying common conditions to life-threatening illnesses. Why does this happen? Because the mind has a powerful effect on the biochemistry of the body. A lot of research has shown that chronic negative emotions cause internal toxic chemical reactions that can be very harmful. Sickness can come in the form of new illnesses or as flare-ups of existing dormant ones. You may have already developed some of the following problems commonly experienced by abused partners:

- Pain or uncomfortable feeling in the stomach, tightness in the throat, pressure in the chest, feeling that you can't breathe.
- Nervousness, internal shakiness, muscle tension, body aches, headaches. Constant state of preparedness.
- Fatigue and exhaustion. (Feeling as if you are "drained," have been "hit by a truck" or "worked over"—especially right after an abusive incident has taken place.)
- Difficulty falling asleep, interrupted or restless sleep, nightmares.
- Substantial weight gain or loss.
- Underactivity or overactivity of the immune system, causing more frequent and more severe viral infections (including colds and flu), primary and secondary bacterial infections, and yeast infections. Other common immune system problems include the development of new allergies, flare-ups of existing ones, and some types of arthritis. Having these problems further compromises the immune system, making a person increasingly vulnerable to an array of more serious immune deficiencies and autoimmune diseases, including some forms of cancer.
- Disorders of other physiological systems of the body including cardiovascular, endocrine, digestive, respiratory, nervous, and muscular. These disorders range from shortness of breath, chronic coughs, and panic attacks to irritable bowel syndrome, hypoglycemia, and diabetes; from skin rashes and TMJ disorders (jaw pain and jaw disk displacement due to tension) to high blood pressure and other vascular and heart conditions. The list goes on and on because a high percentage of body malfunctions and diseases have a substantial emotional component.

The conflicts in your abusive relationship are literally played out on the battlefield of your body, as toxic chemical substances circulate, causing disturbances in your normal functioning. Your unhealthy negative emotions wage a war against your body that it will probably lose. How long it may take for physical breakdowns to occur, and the nature of them, will be determined by a variety of factors including your constitution and genetic predispositions. But make no mistake about it; strong negative emotions that persist over time usually take their toll one way or another.

HOW YOU TRY TO FIX THE "PROBLEM" OF BEING VERBALLY ABUSED

When you are in a verbally abusive relationship, you are forced into "the school of necessity." You try everything you can think of to please your partner, to get him to understand how you feel and how you perceive what is going on, and to stop his hurtful behavior. But your efforts are systematically thwarted.

It is natural to expect that your differences can be worked out in a reasonable and loving manner. But you get frustrated trying to resolve what you perceive as conflicts by using methods that can only be effective in normal, healthy relationships, such as attempting to explain your point of view and understand your partner's view; trying to negotiate, compromise, or adjust; considering what your part in the "problem" may be and acting nicer, trying harder, doing more; apologizing and accepting apologies if they are made. When none of these methods work, out of frustration you may try writing your partner letters, explaining what you think he did not understand when you tried to tell him.

You likely resort to such behaviors as defending, explaining, apologizing, pleading, screaming, demanding, and threatening. You turn your focus away from yourself and toward your partner. You begin watching, judging, managing, controlling, manipulating, anticipating, second-guessing, placating, helping, giving advice, encouraging, and praising—doing anything and everything you think may straighten things out and put an end to the hurtful treatment you are receiving. You may narrow your world to suit him, cutting down the amount of time you spend with other people and limiting activities he objects to. Unfortunately these methods usually backfire, putting you right where he wants you—on the defensive. They only escalate the abuse and intensify your confusion and pain.

Or you may continue to see the people and participate in the activities he objects to, but hide the facts and lie when necessary to cover up what you are doing. This solution doesn't work either. Even if he doesn't find out, living a secretive existence under the thumb of a despot only adds to your feelings of worthlessness, unrespectability, and lack of control.

You may try to convince your partner to go with you to couples therapy. If he is like many abusers, he will become angry at the suggestion and say that *you* are the one who needs therapy—not *him*. He may then become more abusive in an attempt to increase the control he believes he is losing. Or, he may go to therapy either to placate you or to attempt to control what you say and learn. If he goes for these reasons, the chances of his stopping the abuse are slim to none.

If your partner chooses to go to therapy because he wants to change his behavior and save your relationship, the chances are better that he may stop abusing someday. However, overcoming a pattern of abuse and achieving lasting change requires commitment and time. So beware of abusive partners who attend therapy sessions for a few weeks or a couple months and claim to be "cured" of their abusive ways forever.

Because physical abuse always begins with verbal abuse, you must take seriously any threats of harm. If you feel unsure of your safety or are afraid of what might happen, honor your instinct by getting help, getting away from your partner, or preferably both. If verbal abuse escalates and he begins throwing things around or slamming his fist into a door or wall, know that you may be next. In this case, it is important to take immediate steps to protect yourself from possible future physical attacks. Abuse therapists, hotlines, and agencies are available to help.

As upset as you may feel right now being reminded of all the changes you have seen in yourself, you are probably relieved to know that you are not alone in the way you have been thinking, feeling, and acting. Lots of abused people are going through the same things you are. In the next chapter we are going to answer questions that you have probably asked yourself a thousand times.

Chapter 4

Why, Oh Why, Does It Have To Be This Way?

Why does your partner act the way he does? Whose fault is it? And why would he hurt *you,* of all people? The answers to these questions will take you closer to freedom from your pain, confusion, and fear.

WHY IS YOUR PARTNER ABUSIVE?

Although numerous factors can contribute to people becoming abusive, two usually underlie the others. First, they may have innate biological tendencies to behave as they do. We all know that people are born different. Scientific evidence has confirmed that we are all born with a unique combination of inherent traits. Many are apparent in infancy. Some abusive people, for example, may be innately prone to be anxious, hypersensitive, or aggressive. Then their life experiences may make these innate tendencies more pronounced. Patterns of behavior such as aggressiveness and submissiveness are sometimes obvious. A toddler who pushes other children may become a child who bullies, then an adult who abuses. A quiet, sensitive, insecure child may become a self-doubting adult who is a prime target for abuse.

The second reason some people become abusive is because they have a deep reservoir of strong, painful negative feelings—shame, grief, fear, and anger—caused by childhood experiences and unmet childhood needs. Behaving abusively is the way they act out their pain. Their childhood home environments may have ranged from being somewhat strict to outright abusive. They may have been mistreated or overly controlled by parents or other adults, or they may have felt they were.

If they were brought up with abuse, they were taught that they are not okay and that it is not okay to feel what they feel. And they probably witnessed one parent or parent figure regularly abusing the other. If their mother abused them or didn't protect herself or them from their father's abuse, they may have learned to see women as weak or controlling, or both, and hate them for it. Often under these conditions, children develop a distorted view of how relationships work, how to get needs met, and how to cope with emotions. They have confusions about masculinity, women, love, relationships, and personal power. They learn to equate love with pain and masculinity with dominating others—and they learn to distrust.

As these children grow up, if more and more strong negative feelings are stuffed into the bulging reservoir of resentment and pain, the pressure builds much like a volcano. In volatile partners, eruptions occur as a means of relieving the internal pressure created by the powerful pent-up emotions. Subtle abusers relieve the pressure more slowly, venting it a little at a time, more like a simmering teakettle. Both types of abusers act out their suppressed rage by doing what they are prone to do and what they learn to do by example and experience. And the legacy marches on and on.

It is crucial to recognize that although the trigger for your abusive partner's outbursts may seem to be *external*, it is actually *internal*. He uses what you *say* or *do* as an excuse to vent his built-up anger. When he is ready to vent, it doesn't matter whether you are doing or saying anything objectionable. He will find something to abuse you about anyway.

Since nobody is perfect, your partner will occasionally have reason to be upset with you. But even then, when he overreacts and behaves hurtfully, he will not be doing it because of your mistakes, inadequacies, personality, appearance, opinions, reactions, or anything else. The continuous source of fuel for his abusive behavior is his reservoir of old pain. This explains why his reactions are so unpredictable and irrational.

Your partner may try to have control now because he felt out of control as a child, and still does. He may try to feel powerful now because he felt powerless as a child, and still does. He may be trying, once again, to master his powerlessness and lack of control of his world by "working it out" on you and perhaps your children. He may be trying desperately to get it "right" this time, trying *now* to get all he desperately wanted *then*, but didn't get.

Unfortunately, he is not going about it in a way that will ever work. He demands enormous amounts of love and acceptance, approval and appreciation. But no matter how much he gets, he doesn't feel lovable enough or acceptable enough to believe that it is real. Nothing fills the emptiness that he has carried since childhood. His greatest fears are of being rejected or abandoned. Ironically, he sets himself up for rejection and abandonment by behaving abusively to those closest to him, those most likely to give him the love he has always wanted. Right now that is you and perhaps your children.

He uses other people as objects to make himself feel better, and he is so self-consumed that he thinks his concerns are all that matter. Believing his *internal* world is out of control drives your partner to attempt to control his *external* world. He thinks the way to do this is to control and have power over other people—as the adults in his early life had control and power over him.

Unfilled needs, a low opinion of himself, and his gigantic reservoir of old pain cause your partner to have a low frustration tolerance. This means he easily overreacts to new stresses, pressures, or problems in his life. Lacking coping skills, he handles stress by abusing. If he is unhappy at work, is not making enough money, is upset with himself for making a mistake, or if he is dealing with any number of other disappointments or pressures, something as minor as your glancing at another man or a child dropping a toy on the floor is enough to set him off. If he abuses drugs or alcohol—as many abusive partners do in an effort to fill their emptiness and numb their pain—it compounds his problems and further fuels his abusive behavior.

Accustomed to stuffing his feelings instead of dealing with them, your partner may habitually save up his anger toward other people, such as his parents or his boss, and vent it on *you*, instead of confronting and upsetting *them*. In his mind, it's safer.

Regardless of *why* he abuses, the result is the same: You become the dumping ground for your abusive partner's psychological garbage—the diversion he uses to avoid getting to the source of his problems.

Abuse is a bandage that serves as a temporary "fix" for his pain. He gets an immediate release of tension and a momentary "high" when he experiences the control and power he craves. But because the underlying, unresolved issues and feelings are not being dealt with, and because he continues to stuff more negative feelings into his reservoir of old pain, he continues to suffer—and he continues to abuse.

Your partner learns exactly what to say and how to say it to get the control and power he wants. He comes to know how you think, feel, and react. He learns your vulnerabilities and mercilessly uses them to his own advantage. He expertly uses words and behavior as weapons to disarm you—the person he has come to believe is his enemy. You aren't sure why or when he began treating you as if you were his enemy, but you know he is because you often feel as if you are living in a "war zone."

Although he may not be aware of it, your partner's goal is to confuse and weaken you, making you more controllable. To this end, he initiates a continuing undermining of your sense of self, as well as your self-respect, self-worth, self-love, self-confidence, sense of well-being, perceptions, emotional and psychological equilibrium, ability to cope, and a host of other elements basic to mental stability. This process is so insidious that you may not realize it has been happening. And if you were treated with disrespect as a child—as most abused partners were—or grew up seeing one parent dominate and control the other, you may have difficulty recognizing your partner's behavior as anything out of the ordinary, much less abusive. It feels familiar.

So what is the bottom line here? That your abusive partner is acting out the turmoil raging within him by dumping his childhood fury all over you. That he is a big, angry bully who doesn't like himself, who only feels powerful and in control of the world around him when he abuses, and who makes himself feel "one up" by putting you down. And that you become increasingly conditioned to accept this behavior and to believe you are some-how at least partly causing it, especially if you experienced similar treatment as a child.

WHOSE FAULT IS IT, ANYWAY?

You may feel sorry for your abuser when you think about the causes of his abusive behavior. You may begin to believe that they excuse his behavior and that he had little choice other than to become abusive. Well, think again.

Is it sad he may be prone to behave abusively? Yes, but others have the same tendency, yet do not act upon it. Is it sad he was not taught differently, conditioned differently, and did not have a different childhood or different life experiences? Yes, but many of us have had painful pasts and families of origin that taught unhealthy behaviors, yet we don't abuse other people.

Adulthood is when most of us assume responsibility for our behavior in spite of what we may be innately prone to do and what may have happened to us in childhood. Your abusive partner has to be treated like an adult and held accountable for his actions. Responding to demands and rewarding bad behavior with love and loyalty will not make him become a model partner any more than they would make a spoiled, out-of-control child become a model child.

You, too, need to overcome whatever negative innate ten-dencies you may have to feel weak, be subservient, and think in irrational ways. You, too, need to change any learned patterns that keep you stuck in your destructive behavior. So you must stop thinking this minute that if you love your partner enough he will quit abusing you and suddenly become capable of loving you the way you want him to. You cannot control his behavior with your love, no matter how much you shower upon him. He is the way he is. You cannot change him. You cannot fix the part of him that is broken. Don't you think it is time you stop trying to do the impossible and recognize that your partner has choices?

- He can choose to ignore or to deny the problems his behavior creates in his life and in the lives of those he supposedly loves, and continue his abuse.

- He can choose to recognize that his behavior is a problem but blame his heritage, his past, his parents, society, stress, or you, and deem his behavior inevitable and unchangeable.
- He can choose to repeatedly apologize for his behavior and insist time and again that it is getting better, as it continues to grow worse.
- Or he can choose to take responsibility for the havoc he has been wreaking, seek professional help willingly because he wants to stop abusing, and commit himself determinedly until he has worked through the issues that are causing his abusive behavior, and he no longer abuses.

No one has to be a helpless pawn of the past or of his biological tendencies to be disturbed, not even him. It is a choice—*his* choice. So whose fault is it that your partner's behavior is abusive? It is his and his alone. No one *has* to abuse others—not even if he was born biologically prone to do so, not even if he had a horrendous childhood, not even if he is justifiably filled with rage over something past or present, not even if he has overwhelming pressures to deal with, not even if he believes wholeheartedly that you are the cause of his anger, not even if he has not learned how to handle his anger, not even—anything! He *chooses* to abuse, just as you *choose* to remain there and be abused.

You are not responsible for your partner's being abusive. You are not responsible for the reasons *why* he became abusive. And you are not responsible for his choosing *you* to abuse. What you *are* responsible for is that you choose to allow yourself to be the recipient of his abuse and that you allow his abuse to affect you as profoundly as it does.

We all have choices to make in life. One of your partner's choices is to abuse you. And although he probably is not aware of the reasons or motives for his behavior, he *is* aware he is saying and doing things that cause you great pain and adversely affect your relationship. He sees your pain and you have undoubtedly told him how hurtful his treatment of you is. Yet time and again he *chooses* to continue his behavior. He *chooses* not to take responsibility for his actions and not to learn about what is really going on. He *chooses* not to explore or resolve the psychological issues that cause him to behave as he does. He may also abuse alcohol or drugs and *choose* not to recognize his addiction or to do anything to stop it. Even if your partner is a gentle and kind person who doesn't have a malicious bone in his body, and who really does not understand what he is doing "wrong," he can still *choose* to take a long, hard look at his behavior, instead of assuming you are finding fault where there is none. This is all clearly irresponsible behavior.

Don't kid yourself by thinking your partner can't help behaving abusively. He *can* if he *chooses* to. He doesn't abuse his boss, does he? He probably chooses not to abuse most other people outside your home, either. As a matter of fact, those who abuse their partner usually do it behind closed doors and they are perceived by others to be "charming, personable, warm, friendly, nice people."

Whatever the reasons for your partner's abuse, they rest with *him*—not with *you*—even though you are not a perfect person. In a healthy, non-abusive relationship, your weaknesses, insecurities, inadequacies, idiosyncrasies, and vulnerabilities would not be used to attack you. Repeatedly hurting the one you love is *never* justified. This is crucial to remember. You may find it difficult to believe right now, but when you come to see the truth of it, you will have taken a major step toward freedom from abuse.

Once you realize that your partner is *not* a poor victim of his biological heritage, his past, or circumstances beyond his control, you won't fall into the trap of feeling sorry for him or trying to "help him" get better. You will know that the only way he will change is if he chooses to change himself. When you stop trying to fix him, you will have taken another big step toward freedom.

WHY *YOU*?

If your partner's abuse is the result of his own nature and psychological agenda and you are not the cause, then why does he pick on *you*—the one he supposedly loves most? Perhaps he has developed a distorted concept of what a love relationship should be, especially if he grew up in an abusive household or in a culture that accepts treating women like property. Perhaps he believes that being your partner entitles him to treat you any way that suits him; that he has a right to be your owner, master, keeper, judge, jury, and jailer. This may go for the children, as well. Or it could be that you are the target for your partner's anger because you are in a similar role to his mother's or to other women's he may have loved in the past who disappointed, hurt, or abandoned him. When he reacts angrily to you, he may actually be acting out his old anger toward them.

We can go on and on surmising reasons why *you* are the one he abuses, but there are two basic ones. First, you chose to be with him. You may say you didn't know your partner was "like that" until you were already involved with him. Maybe you weren't aware of the behavioral signs that were there. Or maybe you saw some signs but thought they were not important. Or maybe you were attracted to his charm or masculine, "take-charge" personality. Or maybe you chose *him* because he chose *you*. You couldn't resist his intense romancing: his wanting you so much, loving you so much, needing you so much, and telling you that you are beautiful, wonderful, special, a princess beyond compare—all the things you had waited your entire life to hear. Regardless, you brought him into your life, giving him access to you.

The second reason he abuses *you* is because he *can*! Because you are there. Because you stay. Because you take it. Because, on some level, he believes you have too much invested in the relationship to leave. Because he knows that your weaknesses, insecurities, and dire needs keep you locked in. Because you are addicted to his behavioral swings back and forth between love and anger. Because you accept repeated attacks on your self-worth and allow yourself to be demeaned. Because you keep reinforcing his abusive behavior by allowing him to get his power "high" at your expense. Because he knows how very much you will tolerate. But there is good news. These are reasons you can do something about.

Ask yourself, Whom do bullies usually choose to pick on? Do they bully strong people who can stand up to them, or do they bully those who are weak, defenseless, and fearful? Even if you sometimes get up the nerve to tell your partner his behavior is unreasonable and you won't stand for it anymore, he knows you will—that it is an empty threat—because you have said it before, yet you are still there.

You may be behaving weakly and ineffectively in your primary relationship even if you are a strong, capable, assertive, independent woman in other areas of your life and in other relationships. The same thing can happen if you are a man. A surprising number of men, some powerful, successful, and wealthy, are being verbally abused by a woman. For it is in love relationships that we all become truly vulnerable—and our fairy tales of happily ever after, our illusions about love, and our weaknesses, insecurities, dire needs, and perceived powerlessness can do us in.

In the next chapter you will learn what true, healthy love is— and what it is not. And you will test the state of your relationship using some simple, yet amazingly revealing, criteria.

Chapter 5

It Feels Like Love...
But Is It?

How many times have you heard "I wouldn't be so angry if I didn't love you so much" or "I'm only telling you this because I love you so much"? These kinds of statements, and the intensity behind them, deliver very confusing messages. They excuse expressing anger and inflicting pain in the name of love. No wonder abused partners often mistake the powerful connection between themselves and their partners as love, when in fact it is usually something quite different.

Because you and your partner are filled with dire needs from your past and because both of you learned to associate love with anger and pain, these feelings intermingle until you can't tell one from the other. You equate intensity of feeling with love—even when the feeling is pain.

One of the most basic distinctions between abusive and non-abusive relationships is that healthy, non-abusive relationships are fueled by *love,* not *anger.* Abusive relationships, on the other hand, are fueled by *anger,* not *love.* Do you know whether your relationship is love based or anger based?

The difference between a relationship in which love reigns and one in which anger reigns is clearly explained in my (M.G.P.'s) book *The Princess Who Believed in Fairy Tales.* In the following excerpt, the princess's wise, banjo-playing owl guide, Henry Herbert Hoot, D.H. (Doctor of the Heart), explains to her what true love is:

"True love means freedom and growth rather than ownership and limitations. It means peace rather than turmoil, and safety instead of fear," Doc said, beginning to talk faster. "It means understanding, loyalty, encouragement, commitment, connectedness, and—ah, this is an especially important part for *you*, Princess—respect. For when one is not treated with respect, there is often pain; a deep, unsettling, destructive, nerve-frazzling kind that is never a part of the beauty that is true love."

The princess replied, "I know about *that* only too well. And now I know it was my obligation to accept nothing less than respect, but even true love surely must have its difficult moments. I mean, sometimes people get upset and say things…"

"Yes, but one can be upset about something another person says or does without disliking and mistreating the person who said or did it. True love means agreeing to disagree as friends and teammates, rather than as adversaries or competitors, for true love is not about warring or winning." His voice grew louder and deeper, and he stood tall, his chest puffing out like a peacock. "And it is never demeaning, never cruel, never attacking, never violent. It makes a home a castle, never a prison."

WHAT DO THESE RELATIONSHIP TESTS TELL YOU ABOUT YOUR RELATIONSHIP?

Everyday experiences provide you with valuable insight into how you really feel about various aspects of your life. It is important to pay attention to these feelings and learn from them. Feelings are signals meant to alert you that something is or is not working to your benefit. Various situations can bring up feelings that tell a lot about what's going on in your relationship. Here are three interesting ones you may find helpful.

Wedding Test

The same elements expressed by Doc about true love are often expressed in wedding ceremonies. Perhaps you have had the experience of sitting at someone's wedding or watching a wedding in a movie or on television, fighting to hold back tears as you listened to the betrothed being told that they should love, respect, and be devoted to each other, and that they should be each others main source of strength. That their home should be a sanctuary from the world, a haven, a place of serenity and renewal. Did you feel sadness and pain wash over you as you were reminded of the dreams you once had of cherishing your loved one, and of being cherished? Did it seem that all you had hoped for had simply slipped away?

Greetings Card Test

How do you feel while choosing a birthday, anniversary, or Valentine's Day card for your partner? Have you ever read card after card that expressed thanks for being loving, being wonderful, being the light of your life—and put each back with an ache in your heart growing stronger and stronger? Did your chest grow tight and tears well up in your eyes as you realized that the only card you could honestly give to your partner wouldn't say any of those loving things? Did you end up leaving the store broken-hearted and empty handed?

"Our Song" Test

When you hear "your song," do you still feel joyful as you once did? Or do you feel depressed and wonder what went wrong? When you hear songs of love lost, do they make you feel as if you want to cry? Do songs that speak of loving devotion make you ache inside because that's what you expected to have, but don't? Have you turned off the radio wanting to avoid the pain? And did you feel sick at heart anyway?

The Wedding Test, Greetings Card Test, and "Our Song" Test are amazingly reliable ways of discovering your true feelings about your partner and your relationship. (They evolved from the common experiences of eight women who were members of the original "Happily-Ever-After Club"—a remarkable women's therapy group in which I [M.G.P.] participated.)

Here's a statement that will further clarify what your relationship really is—and is not. Use it as a criterion for evaluating relationships in your life.

"Love must be shown in *thought, word,* and *deed*."

Just *saying* he loves you isn't enough. If your partner's thoughts are not loving, if his words are not loving, if his deeds are not loving—consistently—then what you have is not love.

Now think for a moment. Based on all the criteria mentioned so far in this chapter, does your relationship rate as a loving one?

Here are some other important questions to ask yourself:

- Is your well-being your partner's priority?
- Does he accept, like, honor, and respect you as you are?
- Do you accept, like, honor, and respect him as he is?
- Do you accept, like, honor, and respect yourself when you are with him?
- Does he bring out the best in you?
- Is he your best source of emotional support and encouragement?
- Does he believe in you and your abilities?
- Does he encourage your personal growth?
- Do you feel like a separate person with valid opinions, beliefs, and preferences?
- Is he proud of your achievements and accomplishments?
- Do you feel understood, validated, safe, and peaceful?
- Is he your best friend? Consistently?
- Does being with him affirm and enhance your life?
- Are you happy when you are with him?

IT'S TIME TO FACE THE FACTS

Are your eyes filled with tears and your heart filled with sadness after reading the relationship tests and thinking about your answers to the questions above? As difficult as it is to face the truth of your situation, it's the only way out of your pain. So you may feel a little worse before you feel better, but it will be worth it.

If you are in an abusive relationship your partner is *not* interested in straightening out hurtful "misunderstandings." He is *not* interested in discussing the "problem." He is *not* interested in making peace. He is *not* interested in hearing how he is hurting you or in understanding how you feel. He is *not* interested in your welfare or in the welfare of his relationship with you. He is *not* on your side.

He *is* your opponent in a fierce, ongoing mental tug-of-war—a fact he adamantly denies. You can trust neither his behavior toward you nor the things he says to you. He *is* interested in gaining control over you and will use almost any means available to establish and maintain that control, whether or not he realizes that he is doing it. He does whatever it takes to make himself stronger and you weaker, himself more in control and you less in control. His behavior is fueled by *anger*—not *love*. Anger—not love—is the glue that holds your relationship together. And mutual emotional dependence is the foundation of it: you each depend on the opinion and responses of the other for your sense of self.

If you believe you "can't live without him," your relationship is based on necessity, not love. And if your partner is using any means he can to hold on to you—including making you too weak and insecure to leave—he is just as afraid of living without you. This is not love either. The intensity of your feelings may deceive you into believing you are in love, when in fact what you are experiencing is a result of unconscious needs, emotional or sexual addiction, or other problems.

Having a strong desire to be loved and approved of by your partner is quite natural. It is part of the human condition. The researcher John Bowlby and other psychologists have shown that infants are born with a strong tendency to become attached to their parents and other caretakers, to be loving, and to want love in return. As adolescents and adults, we retain this biological tendency. Unfortunately, some of us (especially those with unmet childhood needs) exaggerate our innate tendency into a dire *need* for significant others' love and approval—and we may revolve much of our life around getting this need filled.

Healthy love is based on a *desire* for love and approval, rather than a *need* for it. When you don't get it, you feel sad and disappointed. You are motivated to look for it and to try to bring it into your life, but you do not feel desperate. And when significant others are unloving or emotionally unavailable, you recognize that you are not getting what you want from them and are able to break away and look elsewhere. Healthy love exists only when both partners are fully capable of living their lives without each other but choose to be together. They choose out of strength rather than desperation.

A dire need for love and approval is quite different, and is unhealthy. When it is blocked or replaced with unloving behavior and disapproval, you may convince yourself that because you don't have what you *absolutely need,* it's *awful,* you are *unlovable,* you *don't deserve* love, and perhaps you're generally *worthless.*

When you have a dire need for love and approval and are with an abusive partner, you're *really* in trouble. The more abusively he behaves, the more upset and depressed you become, and the harder you try to "make" him give you the love and approval you crave. Then you become more attached than ever to him and even more dependent on his approval. When he is not being abusive, and is actually nice, you feel as if you are rising to heaven in a golden chariot. When he goes back to being abusive, you get moody and feel depressed.

You may have been through a similar scenario with one or both of your parents or caretakers when you were a child. If so, your desperation to get the one you love to love you back is a repeat of an old struggle that locks you into your relationship and can play tricks with your mind.

Do not be fooled. Remember, your abusive partner is not your friend, even though he sometimes may behave like a friend. He is a wolf in sheep's clothing, a daunting adversary with a well-conceived—although perhaps subconscious—battle strategy. He sets you up by tearing you down, catches you off guard, then zeros in for the kill—again and again. If you allow him to continue, you will become so worn out from fighting battle after battle that you will eventually lose the war—the war to preserve your mental and physical health and to lead a love-filled, joyful life.

Here are more cold, hard facts:

- Verbal abuse is a form of domestic violence. It is a form of psychological and emotional torture. It is a form of brainwashing. It is *never* a form of love.
- The powerful connection between partners in abusive

relationships is usually perceived as love, when actually it is a desperate, mutual emotional dependence.

- Trying to get through rationally to a partner who is behaving irrationally is doomed to failure.
- Verbal abusers who do not get professional help do not get better; they almost always get worse.
- Verbal abuse sometimes escalates to include physical attacks on objects: punching, throwing, ripping, and breaking things. Physical attacks on objects may escalate to physical attacks on a partner.
- Verbal abuse is the first stage of physical abuse. Verbal abuse always precedes and accompanies physical abuse, but many verbally abusive partners never become violent.
- Verbal threats of harm and the brandishing of weapons must be taken seriously.
- When verbal abuse that has been going on in private begins to take place in front of other people, it is often a sign that the abuse is advancing to the next stage—physical abuse.
- Once it is apparent that a physical threat exists, you must take preventive action. Get help and leave. Or, at least, prepare yourself ahead of time in case you ever *have* to leave in a hurry.
- It is much easier to get out of a verbally abusive relationship before you have been in it for years and it has taken a debilitating long-term emotional, psychological, and physical toll on you.

YOU SUFFER AND LEARN AND GET BETTER AND SUFFER SOME MORE

In spite of it all, most abused partners stay and try to make the best of their situation, but unless they do something radically different, they only suffer more. Others leave, thinking it will set them free; and for some it does, but most continue to suffer. While they no longer suffer from the continued attacks of their former Prince Charming, they may suffer from the attacks of the next or the next, while wondering how they could possibly have gotten themselves into the same situation again. Those who leave and do not fall into this common trap may still suffer because of the pain, confusion, fear, and poor self-image that often persist long after they have put time and distance between themselves and their abusive relationship.

Whether they stay or leave, abused partners try many things to stop their suffering. Some bury their head in the sand and bear the pain in solitude. Others read about their situation, talk about it, and join groups. They try to grow, learn, be strong, let go, take good care of themselves, become more spiritual—and it helps. But no matter how much better they get, if they stay in their relationship they still face a daily struggle to repeatedly reestablish and maintain their emotional, psychological, and physical equilibrium.

If they leave, they face years of struggling to get over what they have been through, to finally make sense of it all, to heal their stress-embattled body, to work through the practical challenges and new fears that threaten to overwhelm them when they step out into life on their own, and to change their behavior patterns so they won't get into the same situation with another abusive "Prince Charming."

So is all lost? Are you destined to wallow around in the muck of your life forever? The answer is an unequivocal No! Whether you stay or leave, you can step into each day with confidence, your head held high. You can pat yourself on the back instead of beating yourself up. The moments of your life can glitter like jewels in the sunlight. How do we know? Because we have known many verbally abused women who were tired and sick and confused and sad and lonely and afraid, who are now energetic and stronger and clearer and happier and more fulfilled and secure than they have ever been in their lives. Every day sparkles with the realization that they have chosen to use their experience with abuse as a learning tool to become stronger and wiser. They have chosen to use their inherent power to heal themselves, mend their broken dreams, and reweave the fabric of their lives.

You can do the same. You and these women are of like minds, of like hearts, of like dreams and shattered dreams—princesses all. And you, too, who pinned your hopes for happiness on finding and loving a Prince Charming will discover that the surest way to live happily ever after is to first find and love yourself.

YOUR ABUSE IS A WAKE-UP CALL... WILL YOU ANSWER IT?

Your abuse is a call to wake up your self-respect, your dignity, your self-love, and your personal power. It is a motivator to search for clarity and peace, and an opportunity to grow and blossom as a person—to find out who you are, what life is all about, and what true love is. Abuse can be a door to insight and wisdom or a painful prison from which there seems to be no escape. The choice is yours. And it *is* a choice.

Your relationship is like a mirror, reflecting what you must learn. It can send you searching deep within yourself to find out such things as why you attracted an abusive man, why you react to abuse as you do, and what old emotional wounds have kept you hooked into him and into an unhealthy alliance with pain and suffering. The answers to these queries will bring you face to face with the beliefs that rule your life, and will provide you with the opportunity for personal growth and transformation.

Your emotional pain may seem to be your enemy but it has an important purpose. It's a signal attempting to get your attention, a big red flag waving more and more frantically in your face until it can no longer be ignored. Pain is a catalyst to a better you, a better life. It helps you recognize what you want and pushes you to take the necessary steps to get it. It can force you to grow strong, learn more, and feel better about yourself. You can turn it into something positive in your life and use it to do things you had never thought possible.

You can have what you want more than anything else in the world: to be set free—free from your pain, your confusion, your fear, and your feelings of not being good enough. You can have truth, understanding, and validation. You can be respected, appreciated, and loved. You can regain belief and respect in yourself, find meaning and fulfillment, and discover true, lasting love that doesn't hurt. You can have peace in your head and your heart, and you can learn to believe again that it is really possible to have your happily ever after, after all.

We have all believed in fairy tales about ourselves and our lives that we hoped would come true. Yours still can. It's not too late. It's not impossible. No matter what your past or present problems, you can learn how to turn your difficult experiences into tools that build new dreams. Remember, in every fairy tale there is evil to conquer. The presence of evil doesn't mean the fairy tale cannot come true. It means the evil must be overcome *in order* for the fairy tale to come true. What if Cinderella had been so devastated by the treatment she received for years from her stepmother and stepsisters that she had given up on her herself and her dreams, and had not found the courage to attend the ball? Think about that. How will you ever know what wonderful things may be awaiting you if you give up on yourself and your dreams?

You are stronger than you think you are. Facing the truth about your relationship and yourself takes courage, but you are doing it! You are taking that first crucial step to breaking the bonds of your abuse. Feel good about yourself and give yourself credit for being willing to look objectively at what is going on. It isn't easy. Not every abused partner chooses to do it. You are one of the strong ones, or you wouldn't be reading this book.

The more you learn, the stronger you will become—and the better able you will be to take action that will bring peace to your heart and joy to your life. This book will show you how, step by step. Even if your prince has turned into a toad, you can learn how to live happily ever after. Others have done it. Now you are going to learn the secret of making it happen for you.

PART II

The Secret Revealed

Chapter 6

The Secret
What It Is

Have you come to believe some of the things your abusive partner says about you, no matter how hard you have tried to ignore them? Do you think verbal abuse is responsible for having lowered your self-acceptance and self-worth? That it has sapped your energy, stolen your self-confidence and self-respect, and entrapped you in an endless web of pain? If so, the following indisputable facts may surprise you because they are contrary to what you may believe and what you may have heard and read elsewhere:

- You don't have to hurt badly, no matter what. You don't have to blame yourself or feel guilty or stupid or ugly or bad or lacking or incompetent or responsible for the abuse you are or were receiving. And it doesn't matter whether the negative things your abuser says about you are true, untrue, or somewhere in between, you absolutely do not have to hurt badly over them.
- You have the power to prevent your abusive partner— or anyone else—from turning you into a subservient, confused, fearful, pathetic creature who at times doubts her own sanity.
- You can climb off the emotional roller coaster whether or not your abusive partner changes.
- You have control over your suffering and can stop it.
- You have control over your own peace of mind and happiness and can choose to have them.

Do you find it difficult to believe you can feel enormously better even if you continue to be abused? It would not be surprising if you do. You have undoubtedly already tried various ways of reducing your suffering that have not worked. Trying to be "less sensitive" has not worked, nor has trying to "rise above it." Reminding yourself of the old adage "Sticks and stones may break my bones, but words will never hurt me" has definitely not worked. Even fighting back has not helped you to feel better.

Because these ways have not worked does not mean that *nothing* will work. You have instinctively tried to reduce the severity of your abuser's impact on you by taking charge of your emotions in the ways you knew. Now you are going to learn a different way—a proven way. You do not have to believe it will be effective. You just have to be willing to try it. You have tried everything else. Are you willing to try one more thing? If you are, you can ultimately triumph over your pain.

YOU HAVE GREAT PERSONAL POWER EVEN THOUGH YOU MAY NOT FEEL IT RIGHT NOW

We will show you that although verbal abuse *can* overwhelm you and destroy your happiness and peace of mind—as it does for the majority of abused partners—it is *not* inevitable. You can change the face of your world, even if the world around you remains unchanged. When you learn how to take charge of your emotions, you will realize that you have powers you thought you lost or lacked: the power to control your feelings and your life; the power to decide how you will perceive yourself, your abuse, and your abuser; and the power to decide how you will react to them and deal with them. In fact, you have as much personal power as you believe you have.

If you are a woman of smaller stature and less physical strength than your partner, and if you haven't the skills or experience to financially support yourself, it is understandable that you might think you do not have much power. But some strong, athletic women, and some who have successful careers, also feel helpless in their relationship with their abusive partner. Have you ever thought about what it would take to make *you* feel strong and powerful? Think about it.

Now think about the men who are severely abused by their partner. As amazing as it may seem, they quietly endure their humiliating secret and excruciating pain, the same as women do. Some are ordinary men with ordinary lives; others are extraordinary men with extraordinary lives. There are robust, athletic types and scholarly, intellectual types. Regardless, in their personal life, they are like frightened little boys, allowing themselves to be crushed under the thumb of a critical, domineering mother-like partner.

These men are various combinations of big, strong, financially independent, successful, rich, influential, intelligent, educated, and worldly—all the attributes you may think would help you to have personal power. Nevertheless, they are too afraid to live their lives as they wish. Afraid to do anything to displease their partner for the same reasons you are afraid to displease yours. They are afraid to do anything but helplessly and silently stand by while their abusive partner controls or misuses their money, controls their time and activities, turns their children against them, makes them a last priority, and berates them mercilessly—perhaps in front of other people as well as in private. Even those who resort to living secret private lives so they can escape some of their partner's scrutiny live in constant fear of her irrational behavior and vendettas. They allow themselves to be held hostage by their fear of her wrath.

We have known such men and tried to help them see that their powerlessness is a result of how they perceive themselves. Because they are physically strong and financially independent, you would expect them to have great personal power and to be good at managing their lives. But *personal power is a state of mind.* This is important to remember. Although you may feel powerless in your relationship, you are, in truth, only powerless if you choose to give up your power to your partner. If you see yourself as weak, you will be weak. If you see yourself as strong, you will be strong.

Now pay close attention. You are about to learn the first of seven basic truths that can change your life. These truths are the foundation of the secret of overcoming verbal abuse. It may be difficult at first to read some of these truths—you may want to scream at us for saying them—but they are the key to your feeling better.

Basic Truth #1
You, and *only you*, create your feelings.

As incredible as it sounds, the devastating emotions you attribute to being verbally abused are of your own making. In fact, *all* your emotions are of your own making. No one can *make* you feel *anything*. *You* make you feel every emotion you experience. You also are in control of the intensity of each emotion you experience. Your abuser does not have the power to hurt you with his words and behavior—not without your help. No one can *make* you feel *anything* without your permission, without your participation.

So as much as you might believe your abusive partner is to blame for all your pain, the truth is that the most painful emotional hoops you continuously jump through are of your own creation. Although you may not want to hear this, it is wonderful news. Why? Because it means you can do something to stop the pain without having to rely on your abuser to stop it for you! Did you get this? It is going to turn out to be the best news you have heard in a long time. Here it is again: *You can do something to stop the pain without having to rely on your abuser to stop it for you.*

You no longer have to feel out of control and compelled to explain, urge, beg, manipulate, or try to force your abuser to stop the pain for you. *You* can stop your pain. In fact, *you* are the only one who can! You are the one person, the *only* person, who has the power to change *you*. You can do more to diminish your pain than can anyone else on earth—including your abusive partner. If you decide to put the enormous energy you have been wasting on trying to fix him into fixing yourself instead, you can greatly reduce your suffering, take back your personal power, and make yourself and your life feel good again.

That is why the rest of this book is primarily about you, rather than your abusive partner. In previous chapters you learned what *he* does—makes himself feel "more than" by trying to make you feel "less than" and uses his big bag of abuse tricks to control you.

You already know what *he* is—an insecure, immature, control freak misogynist who is perhaps also a rageaholic. You already know he can be as irresistible as he is irritating and as loving as he is hateful. You already know that few abusers change, no matter what their partners say or do, or don't say or do. So it is time to face the fact that what your abuser says, does, thinks, and feels is not your main problem, nor should it any longer be your main focus. *You* are your main problem, and it is time for *you* to be your main focus.

Although you never planned to, you have unwittingly become partners with your abuser. When he isn't busy abusing you, you abuse yourself. You become the abuser you can't ever get away from. The abuser who knows every one of your weaknesses and inadequacies; who remembers your mistakes, blunders, most embarrassing moments, foibles, and idiosyncrasies, and who is expert at using them against you and helping others to use them against you too. You are the abuser who can badger you and beat you up unmercifully, as often and for as long as she wishes. The abuser whose insecurities, self-doubts, and dire needs make you easy prey for abuse by your partner.

This book was written about *you*, the abuser you can do something about. The abuser who *really* holds the power. And it was written to teach you about this power—the great, innate, life-changing power that is available to you if you will only learn how to use it. Power that can turn the tables of control if you want to stay—or believe you need to stay—in your abusive relationship. Power that can make you strong enough to leave, if that is what you choose. Power to make your dreams come true.

HOW YOU CREATED THE FEELINGS THAT TURNED YOU INTO YOUR OWN ABUSER

As the groundwork for your abusive partner's feelings and behavior were laid in his past, so the groundwork for your feelings and behavior—which includes your abuse of yourself—were laid in your past. When you were young, your mind was programmed much like a computer. But unlike a computer, which is programmed by specialists who have the necessary skills, you had input from imperfect people who had imperfect child-rearing skills.

As a dependent little person without the experience or judgment to think for yourself, you—like most children—gullibly agreed with things that were said and taught to you by these fallible human beings. And you may have taken routine child-rearing guidance and reasonable parental rules and standards and exaggerated them into absolutistic *shoulds* and *musts* about yourself, others, and the world. What you think about everything is based on your evaluations and interpretations of the things you have been told, the way you have been treated, and the experiences you have had.

Unfortunately, as a child, you were unaware that the way you were treated and talked to may have said more about your parents or caretakers and their problems than it did about you. For example, if you had an overworked, impatient mother who coped with stressful situations by yelling, you may have thought *you* were the only reason she was upset, and felt bad about yourself because of it.

Little by little, without realizing it, you made your parents' or other caretakers' judgments, your judgments. The demands they once made on you, you learned to place on yourself. Now that these people are no longer with you all the time dictating your behavior, you stand in for them. You see yourself in the same light they saw you. You treat yourself as they treated you, saying and doing to yourself the same kinds of things they once said and did. And, you tend to live out your parents' expectations of you, whether those expectations are high or low.

To make matters worse, you—and everyone else—have an innate tendency to hold on to the past and to keep it alive for many years, possibly for a lifetime, influencing adult feelings and behavior. Some people become perfectionistic high achievers; others simply give up; and most end up somewhere in between, doing the best they can not to allow their insecurities to hold them back or make them miserable. But far too many go through their lives causing their own pain by saying things to themselves like "I'm so stupid. I should have known that." "This *has to* work out, or I'll just die." "I look so fat in this I *can't stand it.*" So you can see that even if you were raised in a "normal" family, you may have learned to abuse yourself.

Children raised in abusive families are even more likely to be given negative messages. They are told repeatedly in many ways how lacking they are. They are systematically programmed to let a "loved one" tell them what to think, say, do, and feel—and to stuff their frustration and anger about it. If you are in an adult abusive relationship, you were probably mistreated as a child. Perhaps you were told time and again you were not very smart or attractive or good or worthwhile or lovable or capable of doing anything "right" or well enough—or worse. You may have accepted these opinions of yourself, exaggerated them, and come to strongly believe they were true. Once you adopted these beliefs, your perception of yourself was set. From then on, you not only accepted this nonsense about yourself, you unwittingly helped perpetuate it, "feel" that it was true, and act on it—perhaps by living a life of failure after failure.

Your mistreatment may have been blatant, or so subtle you still have difficulty recognizing it. It may have been severe or mild. Regardless, whether or not you are aware of it, you have probably had a lot of practice doubting yourself, feeling bad about yourself, and struggling to get the love and acceptance you think you need. And you are used to trying to get it from people who cannot or will not give it to you, or who give it sporadically and conditionally, alternating love and pain.

You may have seen your mother being abused and learned your role from her. Now you view abusive relationships as normal. You have learned that love often hurts and have become accustomed to dramatic relationships that feel loving one minute and hurtful the next. And here you are again, as an adult, feeling confused, anxious, angry, unsure of yourself, and not good enough to be loved. The less acceptance and love you got as a child, the more you probably think you need now. The depth of your need makes you vulnerable to getting into a hurtful relationship—and to staying in it. No wonder you turned into your own abuser. And no wonder you are where you are now—settling for a life of chaos and pain.

What can you do to stop perpetuating the old thoughts, feelings, and behaviors that keep you in pain? You can change your programming.

CHANGE YOUR PROGRAMMING
CHANGE YOUR LIFE

Perhaps when you reflect on your childhood it seems inevitable that you would have the beliefs, thoughts, feelings, and behavior you do now. But your past could have affected you differently than it did. In fact, you may have brothers or sisters who have a different view than you do of what it was like to grow up in your family, and they may have become very different kinds of adults than you are. What you experienced was partly a result of the view you took of the things that happened to you.

We all know that people see their experiences differently and are affected differently. The same conditions and obstacles that defeat some people spur others on to great accomplishments. One person's half-empty glass is another person's half-full one. Taking another view can change everything. This leads us from the first basic truth—*You* and *only you* create your feelings—to the second basic truth.

Basic Truth #2
Your view of a person, situation, or event determines your reality of it.

Suppose you are in an elevator and ask a man in front of you to please step aside to let you out, but he ignores you. Wouldn't you be annoyed? Maybe even indignant? You might make a sarcastic remark and push past him. But what if you then realized he was deaf and had not heard your request? Wouldn't your feelings completely change?

Wouldn't you suddenly feel understanding and empathetic? Maybe even guilty for your thoughts and behavior? Why would your feelings change when the incident remained the same? Because your view, or interpretation, of the incident changed—and therefore so did the things you were telling yourself about it. This brings us to the third basic truth.

Basic Truth #3
People, situations, and events do not upset you. It is your interpretation of them and what you tell yourself about them that cause you to become upset.

As you have seen, you upset yourself by your *interpretation* of situations, events, and what people say and do. Your interpretation takes the form of thoughts, usually expressed in mental statements. This means that when you think, you usually talk to yourself silently in your own head. The things you tell yourself are what create your emotions and influence your behavior. You literally feel the way you think, and you act the way you feel.

Your thoughts, emotions, and behavior are integrated and interdependent. In almost any situation, as in our elevator example, if you change your interpretation and tell yourself different things, your feelings will change. When your feelings change, your behavior will also change. This is the fourth basic truth.

Basic Truth #4
Thinking produces feelings, which generate behavior.

Now you understand that your feelings and behavior are created by your thinking (which includes your interpretations and the things you tell yourself). Your thinking is based on the beliefs and attitudes you have. Your beliefs and attitudes generally come from your childhood experiences. But your childhood experiences were colored by your innate tendencies to interpret them in a particular way and to think in a particular manner. Even your ability to think rationally has a biological component.

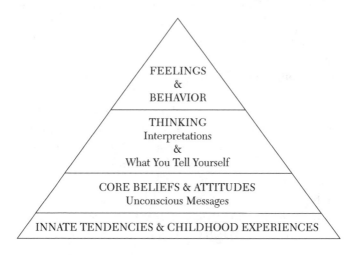

You can readily see that your present feelings and behavior are based on the foundation of your innate tendencies and your childhood experiences. Both resulted in your forming a particular set of beliefs and attitudes that influence how you perceive everything that happens to you. It is through the filter of your basic beliefs that you see yourself and your world. These basic beliefs are called core beliefs; and usually you are not aware of having them. Nonetheless, they influence what you tell yourself about most things in life. And what you tell yourself is mainly responsible for creating your feelings and behavior. This brings us to the fifth basic truth.

Basic Truth #5
Your view of yourself, others, and everything
that happens to you is filtered through
the screen of your beliefs.

To this day, unless you have done something to change them, the same beliefs you adopted in childhood still serve as the foundation of your decisions, choices, perceptions, reactions, feelings, and behavior. Some of these beliefs are responsible for getting you—and keeping you—in an abusive relationship. They are responsible for your staying and settling for crumbs. They are responsible for your abusing yourself. They are responsible for the depth of your suffering. They are responsible for the discomfort that may follow you even if you leave your partner. They are responsible for your continuing insecurities, self-doubts, and dire needs for love and approval that sabotage your relationships and your life.

These beliefs are the culprits that keep you trapped and hurting whether you stay or leave your abusive relationship, and in spite of your newly acquired knowledge and best efforts to improve things. The road out of your pain is to change these core beliefs that are the foundation of your feelings and behavior.

Some of your beliefs were valid at the time you formed them and still are; some were once valid but no longer are; and some were not valid in the first place. Some beliefs are life-enhancing, while others are life-diminishing. Some beliefs are helpful, while others are destructive. Whatever your beliefs are, they are working diligently at running your life, often below your level of awareness. Your beliefs will grow stronger with each passing year unless you take the following actions:

- Listen to what you are telling yourself (that causes you to think, feel, and behave as you do).
- Become aware of the beliefs and attitudes that cause you to think the way you do.
- Reexamine them based on new information you have as an adult.
- Redecide whether they are valid and serve your well-being.
- Change those that are not valid and do not serve your well-being.

The bottom line is that your outdated, invalid, destructive, irrational core beliefs *must* be changed if you are to put a lasting stop to your pain, confusion, and fear, and get your runaway emotions and your life under control. How can you change beliefs you have held for a lifetime? By challenging the programming that created them and perpetuates them. Can you really do it? Yes, you *programmed* yourself—and you can *reprogram* yourself. Updating your mind programming is a skill you can learn. Millions of people have learned the secret of doing it, and so can you.

THE SECRET OF OVERCOMING VERBAL ABUSE
AND ALMOST ANYTHING ELSE

If you are one of the countless women who has been kicked off her pedestal and stomped on as she lies, stunned, on the ground; or one of those who has pulled herself up again and is walking through life still somewhat dazed and hurting, this is the secret you have been waiting for—the one we have been talking about that will help you overcome verbal abuse. It is Rational Emotive Behavior Therapy (REBT), the fastest, most effective, most lasting method ever developed to update your mind programming, take charge of your emotions and your life, and make it possible to no longer be desperately, overwhelmingly upset about your abuse—or anything else. REBT is straightforward and deceptively simple. It is the secret weapon that can end the war within yourself and within your relationship. It is the eternal peacemaker—in your heart and in your life.

REBT has become one of the two most popular forms of therapy in the world. The other is the closely related Cognitive Behavior Therapy (CBT). Both primarily use thinking and reasoning to help people with their emotional problems. The reason for the popularity of these therapies is clear: They are brief, deep, intense, enduring, proven methods that help people reveal and change the basic ideas or philosophies that underlie their disturbing feelings and unwanted habits and behavior.

(The basic concepts of REBT and CBT stem from my [A.E.'s] clinical work and writings. My experiences as a psychotherapist, marriage and family counselor, and pioneer sex therapist led me to question traditional methods of treating emotional disturbances. I observed that in these approaches people gained insight into themselves but did not necessarily learn how to solve their problems. I originated REBT to get to the root of problems—the old, outdated, unhealthy irrational beliefs people hold that cause them to view themselves and their world in ways that cause them pain. These beliefs are revealed, challenged, disputed, and replaced with new, healthy rational beliefs that reduce upsetting negative feelings and pave the way for REBT's practical problem-solving techniques. This unique therapy system includes behavioral homework assignments to help people change their unwanted habits and behavior.)

REBT emphasizes your responsibility for creating your own upsetting emotions and recognizes your ability to reprogram yourself and choose a relatively problem-free, emotionally satisfying life. It is the one system of therapy that separates healthy negative emotions from unhealthy negative emotions and shows you how to create healthy emotions and minimize unhealthy ones.

It holds that *reasoning* is the key to thoroughly and permanently changing your disturbed feelings, because a large element of destructive emotion stems from unrealistic, illogical, and self-sabotaging thinking. REBT shows you how to find the thoughts that underlie your emotional upsets and how to uncover and change your core beliefs—the "unconscious messages" you transmit to yourself that are at the root of your distress.

More than most other schools of therapy, REBT incorporates a wide variety of techniques. It encourages you to use various physical methods—such as relaxation techniques, yoga exercises, and movement therapy—to help yourself feel better while you are learning and using the many REBT cognitive (thought), emotive (emotional) and behavioral techniques.

REBT can help you build yourself emotionally and psychologically strong enough to withstand the rigors of abuse, with its insidious chipping away at your competence, your sense of self, your self-worth, and your emotional and psychological well-being. It can dramatically reduce the intensity of your negative feelings. It can help you stop buying into your partner's abuse and stop compounding it by abusing yourself. It can prepare you to confront your partner in a way that can work. It can help you conquer the fears that keep you trapped, and if you leave, it can help prevent you from getting into another abusive relationship. Whether you stay or leave, REBT can help heal your pain and provide the foundation for a happier, healthier, fuller life.

In the next chapter you will learn how to use REBT to greatly reduce your emotional pain and mobilize your innate power to determine the level of your own happiness and peace of mind.

SUMMARY OF THE FIRST FIVE LIFE-CHANGING REBT BASIC TRUTHS

1. *You*, and *only you*, create your feelings.
2. Your view of a person, situation, or event determines your reality of it.
3. People, situations, and events do not upset you. It is your interpretation of them and what you tell yourself about them that cause you to become upset.
4. Thinking produces feelings, which generate behavior.
5. Your view of yourself, others, and everything that happens to you is filtered through the screen of your beliefs.

Chapter 7

How the Secret Works
The ABCs of Being Rational In An Irrational Relationship

Some people live with partners who repeatedly put them down with the vilest of language, but they recognize that these partners have their own disturbances. They edit out most of their abuser's words, feel displeased, and are able to go about their business with relatively little difficulty. Other people are mildly criticized by their partners and take it all so seriously that they are in constant agony. This shows that it is not so much *what* is said to you by your partner that really upsets you, as it is *how* you *hear* it and *take* it. He is still responsible for his cruel words and deplorable behavior, but *you* are largely responsible for your overreacting to them.

Penny was an REBT client who was sick and tired of feeling miserable every time her husband, Jack, criticized her. She knew she had always been sensitive, but she didn't know what to do about it. In therapy she realized that she felt like the same vulnerable little girl when Jack criticized her as she had years before when she was criticized by her mother and father—and she had believed every word.

She began listening to what she was telling herself while Jack was abusing her. She was surprised to hear the same little girl voice she had used long ago coming out of her adult mouth: "But you don't understand. Please listen to me...." It was a revelation when she realized that when Jack was upset with her, she had been reacting as if he and her parents were all upset with her at the same time. Then there were four of them who didn't think she was good enough—her mother, her father, her husband, and *herself*! When Penny found out that her old irrational beliefs were still whirling around in her mind and had been joined by new irrational beliefs and thoughts, and that they were all talking at once, she understood why she had been so upset.

Her little girl feelings had followed her into adulthood. But she wasn't a little girl anymore and she no longer had to believe the bad things her parents—or her husband—said about her. She no longer had to believe the bad things she said about herself either. Armed with this information and the knowledge that Jack's mistreatment of her wasn't being caused by who she is or what she says or does but by his reservoir of old pain, Penny took a new view of what was happening to her.

Next, she needed a way to act on all she had learned. The ABCs of Emotions started her in the right direction by showing her that she could quiet her unhealthy, irrational mind chatter by replacing it with healthy rational thoughts that would make her feel better. She could hardly believe that after years of being easily hurt and thinking there was nothing she could do about it, she had found the answer. You, too, can learn how to feel better by learning the ABCs of Emotions and changing your irrational beliefs and thoughts the REBT way.

IT'S AS EASY AS A-B-C

In REBT, each of the steps that lead to an emotional reaction is assigned a descriptive letter of the alphabet. This is called the ABCs of Emotions or the ABCs of REBT. It is the basis of REBT. Now we are going to take what you have already learned and put it into REBT terminology.

Something happens. Your partner criticizes you, for example. You react. You become defensive or angry, feel hurt or guilty. It may *seem* as if the criticism caused your feelings. However, as you have learned, being criticized was not the cause. Your attitude or belief about being criticized and the resulting things you said to yourself are what caused you to become upset.

The ABCs of Emotions

- *A* stands for Activating event (something happens).
- *B* stands for Beliefs and thoughts (what you tell yourself about the event).
- *C* stands for emotional and behavioral Consequence (how you feel and act as a result of what you tell yourself).

As you can see, A does not cause C. Rather, B causes C. What determines your emotional and behavioral reaction to an event is not the event itself, but what you tell yourself about it. If you have rational beliefs and thoughts, you will tell yourself rational things. Then your emotions and behavior will be appropriate, realistic, and helpful. If you have irrational beliefs and thoughts, you will tell yourself irrational things. Then your emotions and behavior will be inappropriate, exaggerated, and harmful to you.

Irrational beliefs are unreasonable ideas that cannot be proven. Rational beliefs are sensible, logical ideas that accurately reflect what is happening. It is easy to confuse the two because irrational beliefs often seem valid until you look at them closely. Just *believing* that something is true or logical doesn't make it so.

Here is an example of how the ABCs of Emotions work:

- A (*Activating event*) Your abusive partner criticizes you.
- B (*Beliefs and thoughts*) What you tell yourself about your partner criticizing you.
  "It's *not fair* that he picks on me this way!"
  "It's *horrible* that he's so mean to me!"
  "He *shouldn't* treat me this way. I *can't stand it* one more minute!"
  "There is some truth to what he said. I must *deserve* his criticism."
  "I couldn't think of the right thing to say—again! I'm *stupid* and *worthless*."
  "*Nobody* will *ever* really love me."
- C (*Consequence*) Emotional: defensiveness, anger, pain, shame, guilt. Behavioral: crying, compulsiveness, irritability.

Let's take a close look at this example. When your abusive partner criticizes you, at point A, if you have thoughts similar to those at point B, you probably experience unhealthy negative emotions like those listed at point C. Almost anyone who made these statements and believed them would become upset. If you are criticized harshly and often, and you say such things to yourself each time, you have probably begun to feel more extreme, more lasting negative emotions, such as anxiety, depression, hopelessness, and worthlessness. A goal of REBT is to help you change your irrational beliefs to rational ones, thereby reducing extreme negative emotions to more tolerable ones.

The way to gain control of how you feel and act is to change the disturbing, irrational, unrealistic thoughts that cause your feelings and actions. When you think by *reason,* you will no longer be jerked around by your fluctuating emotions.

YOU CAN HAVE A 10 TO 25 PERCENT DROP IN YOUR EMOTIONAL DISTRESS RIGHT NOW

As we explained in chapter 6, it is your interpretation of the things that happen to you that ultimately cause your emotional reaction. You are probably not aware of the process because your mind works at lightening-fast speed. You may have spent years—perhaps your entire life—being buffeted about and emotionally at the mercy of others. All because you believe that you have *no choice* about the emotions you feel. This one widely held irrational belief alone causes up to 25 percent of emotional distress, according to Maxie C. Maultsby, Jr., M.D., a widely known and respected pioneer and innovator in the field of rational therapy and its scientific basis. His research has shown that just learning the ABCs of Emotions can cause an *immediate,* almost *automatic* 10 to 25 percent drop in emotional distress.

How can this be? Once people learn that much of their emotional distress is their own choice, they start using common sense to think of ways to help reduce their painful feelings. It is that simple.

You can have a 10 to 25 percent drop in your emotional distress by frequently reminding yourself of the ABCs of Emotions you have just learned. Notice how you feel in various situations and listen to the things you are saying to yourself that are causing those feelings. You may be surprised at how easily you can change what you are saying and make yourself feel better. Changing "I can't stand this one more minute" to "There he goes again, acting like a jerk" helps you see the situation rationally rather than emotionally. As you learn to rephrase the statements you make to yourself, you will notice that you become less and less upset both during your partner's outbursts and afterward. Taking charge and refusing to create pain over his behavior will begin to improve the quality of your life right away.

WHAT ABOUT THE REMAINING 75 TO 90 PERCENT OF EMOTIONAL DISTRESS?

Okay, you are off to a good start. Now let's talk about the remaining 75 to 90 percent of your emotional distress that is deeply entrenched in old programming and is habitual. This is the kind of distress that is the main focus of psychotherapy, including REBT. Lasting change comes from getting rid of these old irrational beliefs and replacing them with new rational ones, which REBT is highly effective at accomplishing.

First, you need to learn the REBT techniques for changing your irrational beliefs and thinking. This does not require extensive psychological knowledge and can usually be mastered in a relatively short time. There is an old adage that reflects REBT philosophy: "Give a man a fish and you feed him for a day. Teach him how to fish and you feed him for a lifetime." In fact, if you were to go to an REBT therapist, you would be taught how to become self-sufficient with the same REBT principles and techniques you are learning from this book.

Second, you need to use REBT techniques to become aware of and stop destructive irrational thinking, and to identify your destructive irrational beliefs and fully and permanently change them into constructive rational ones.

Changing old beliefs takes varying amounts of time and effort because there are individual differences in the stubbornness of the beliefs and in people's ability to apply what they have learned. But even the most resistant, automatic, self-defeating habits can be changed in time. Learning how to feel better and how to cope effectively is a process that will forge ahead as long as you diligently, persistently, and determinedly practice, practice, practice the techniques in this book, evaluate your results, and practice, practice, practice some more.

Does this sound like too much work? Think of how much work it takes now just to get through each day. If you use REBT techniques as tools to build a new emotional life, soon your emotional pain will lessen, and the time will come when you will be free.

HOW TO GET RID OF UPSETTING
HABITUAL THINKING

REBT holds that if you want to thoroughly and permanently change your disturbed feelings, it is essential to use your ability to think and reason. Changing unrealistic, illogical, and self-sabotaging thinking to realistic, logical, self-enhancing thinking will get rid of the old habits and programming that keep you in a destructive *thinking* rut—and in a destructive *emotional* rut.

Before going on to the sixth REBT Basic Truth, let's review the first five, which you learned in the last chapter.

1.   *You*, and *only you*, create your feelings.
2.   Your view of a person, situation, or event determines your reality of it.
3.   People, situations, and events do not upset you. It is your interpretation of them and what you tell yourself about them that cause you to become upset.
4.   Thinking produces feelings, which generate behavior.
5.   Your view of yourself, others, and everything that happens to you is filtered through the screen of your beliefs.

Now here is the sixth basic truth that can change your life.

Basic Truth #6
You keep painful feelings alive by repeating your upsetting thoughts to yourself over and over again.

Feelings cannot survive without being continuously fed by thoughts. This is important to remember. When you stop thinking extremely upsetting thoughts and replace them with less upsetting ones, you will feel less upset. It may seem that thinking your way out of emotional distress and destructive patterns of behavior is too simplistic. But the most valuable truths are often very simple. *Crooked* thinking causes emotional distress and *straight* thinking puts an end to it. This brings us to the seventh basic truth.

Basic Truth #7
You can change your feelings and behavior by changing the underlying beliefs and thinking that create them.

How can you change your underlying irrational beliefs and crooked thinking? By using REBT techniques of questioning and challenging your unrealistic, illogical, and self-sabotaging thoughts. You dispute them (designated by the letter D); then replace them with rational, constructive, sensible thoughts, which cause constructive rather than destructive emotions and behavior. (These new rational thoughts are called an effective new philosophy, designated by the letter E.) Now let's review the ABCs of Emotions and see how these two new steps fit into the process.

- *A* stands for Activating event (something happens).
- *B* stands for Beliefs and thoughts (what you tell yourself about the event).
- *C* stands for emotional and behavioral Consequence (how you feel and act as a result of what you tell yourself).
- *D* stands for Disputing of irrational beliefs and thoughts.
- *E* stands for Effective New Philosophy (rational new beliefs and thoughts that reduce negative feelings and actions).

You have learned that thinking, feeling, and behaving are interdependent. You have also learned the REBT Basic Truths and the ABCs of Emotions. If you remember what you have learned and use it in your everyday life, you will notice that you do not get as upset as you used to, or as often, and that your upsetting feelings don't last as long.

In the next chapter you will learn how to dispute the habitual, automatic thinking that causes your painful emotions and inability to cope effectively with your abuse. With effort and practice, you will become proficient at being able to stubbornly *refuse* to be miserable about your partner's abuse. You will *do* better, but that's not all. You will *get* better. You will not only be less *disturbed*, but less *disturbable*. You will be in control of your emotions and be able to confront your partner with clarity and conviction. You will truly be empowered to overcome verbal abuse—and just about anything else.

SUMMARY OF THE LIFE-CHANGING REBT BASIC TRUTHS

1. *You*, and *only you*, create your feelings.
2. Your view of a person, situation, or event determines your reality of it.
3. People, situations, and events do not upset you. It is your interpretation of them and what you tell yourself about them that cause you to become upset.
4. Thinking produces feelings, which generate behavior.
5. Your view of yourself, others, and everything that happens to you is filtered through the screen of your beliefs.
6. You keep painful feelings alive with your upsetting thoughts by repeating them to yourself over and over again.
7. You can change your feelings and behavior by changing the underlying beliefs and thinking that create them.

PART III

Using the Secret to
Set Yourself Free

Whether You Want to Stay,
Need to Stay,
or Plan to Leave

Chapter 8

Getting Off the Emotional Roller Coaster

You know that your partner really *is* verbally abusive, that you are not imagining it. But you are in the driver's seat because your pain is more a result of your thoughts than it is of his behavior. The fact that you are in control of your feelings is great news. But how can you make your life better when the pain never seems to stop? When your partner points out your failings when they exist and invents them when they don't? When he blames you for everything that goes wrong? If the car has a dead battery, it's your fault. If he cuts himself shaving, that's your fault too.

The complaints go on and on. You know the scenarios well. Your partner does his damage, then leaves to go about his day or rolls over and goes to sleep. You feel as if you were hit by a truck. And you continue to upset yourself even when he isn't there.

Must it be this way forever? Not if you change the automatic thinking that causes your pain. You have a choice of how you make yourself feel when "bad" things happen to you (as many philosophers have pointed out over the centuries, and as the existentialists have especially noted in the 20th century). Do you have a complete choice? No, not exactly, for as we have said, you have biological, environmental, and other human limitations. But you still have *some* degree of real choice. When you are treated badly and unfairly, you can choose to feel either healthy negative emotions or unhealthy negative emotions or both about this abuse.

The question is, what feelings are you going to choose to have about your situation? How about disappointment and regret instead of despair and anguish? With your knowledge of REBT's Basic Truths and your soon-to-be-learned REBT skills, you can choose a truly healthy reaction, instead of an unhealthy one, to an obnoxious and unfair situation.

You can choose to feel sorry and disappointed rather than depressed and angry. You can convince yourself that your partner's barrages of hurtful words are bad (and certainly not good) but they are just *too bad,* and not *devastating.* In fact, they are very irrational, intimidating, and insidious—but still only too bad, and not intolerable. Highly obnoxious and unfortunate—but only regretful, only disappointing.

How can you ever convince yourself of this? Start by treating your abusive situation as if it is a problem that requires a "thinking" solution. Recognize that you normally, and sometimes easily, solve practical problems in your everyday life, solve emotional problems that are not related to your abusive relationship, and help other people solve their problems. You are able to problem solve because you are a natural born constructivist. This means you have the ability to think, to think about your thinking—and even to think about thinking about your thinking. It is how you ordinarily survive, and how you ordinarily help yourself get more of what you want and less of what you don't want.

But when it comes to your abusive relationship, you may feel so mixed-up that you have difficulty accessing this innate ability. Now is the time to change this pattern. The key is to recognize that you are separate from your abuser and remind yourself of this fact when he begins his antics. You can learn not to react to everything he says, does, and feels. Every time he gets a look on his face, you don't have to get a pain in your stomach.

THE DIFFERENCE BETWEEN HEALTHY AND UNHEALTHY NEGATIVE EMOTIONS

Most abused partners unknowingly choose to feel unhealthy negative emotions, such as anguish, anxiety, depression, rage, self-hatred, and self-pity. These are destructive and self-sabotaging. They create doubt and indecision, and force you to stay in your relationship when you truly may want to leave. They paralyze your ability to sensibly decide how to act in your own best interest and cause you problem after problem.

Healthy negative emotions such as sorrow, regret, disappointment, frustration, and annoyance are better choices. They are constructive and helpful because they allow you to remain calm and think more clearly. They make it easier to deal effectively with the bad things that happen to you, change or improve the ones you can, and cope with the rest with the least amount of upset feelings possible. You can learn how to have these healthy negative emotions instead of unhealthy negative ones. Then you will feel only sorry and frustrated—although perhaps *very* sorry and *greatly* frustrated—about the abuse.

Once you achieve this healthy negative state, you can sensibly choose to stay and put up with your partner, to leave, or to throw him out. Although emotions like sorrow, disappointment, and frustration are still negative rather than positive, they are healthy because they are appropriate, are based on rational perceptions, serve to alert you to possible danger, and prompt you to take action to protect yourself. They do not immobilize you as unhealthy emotions do. Now think for a moment. Which set of emotions would you rather live with?

We are not suggesting that REBT will make you happy about your abuse, nor is making you happy about it an REBT goal. Even if it were possible, it would be inappropriate and counterproductive. But by becoming aware of the REBT message you can become happier with yourself and your life—in spite of being abused. You can greatly reduce your pain while substantially increasing your ability to deal with it. Just because your partner stuffs a backpack with garbage doesn't mean that you have to carry it around!

So how can you use REBT to make yourself feel healthy negative emotions rather than unhealthy ones? Let's use the ABCs of Emotions to find out.

Thinking in Demands, Musts, and Absolutes Creates *Unhealthy* Negative Emotions

- A *(Activating event)* You are being verbally abused by your partner.

- B *(Beliefs and thoughts about A)*
  "My partner absolutely *must* stop abusing me!"
  "He *can't* treat me this way! It's cruel and unfair!"
  "I'm *stupid* for having gotten into this *horrible, impossible* situation."
- C *(Consequence of A+B) Unhealthy* negative feelings of anguish, anxiety, depression, rage, self-hatred, and self-pity.

Preferential, More Moderate Thinking Creates *Healthy* Negative Emotions

- A *(Activating event)* You are being verbally abused by your partner.
- B *(Beliefs and thoughts about A)*
  "I very much dislike being abused and I wish he would stop."
  "I'd be so much happier if he would just be nicer to me."
  "It's unfair, but lots of things in life are."
  "It would have been better if I hadn't gotten myself into this situation, but we all make mistakes."
- C *(Consequence of A+B) Healthy* negative feelings of frustration, strong disappointment, and sadness.

Compare point B in the two examples above. Notice that when the things you say to yourself about being verbally abused include demands, musts, and absolutes, they create unhealthy negative emotions, as in point C in the first example. These emotions are extreme and very painful. Then notice that when the things you say to yourself are preferential, more moderate beliefs, they create healthy negative emotions, as in point C in the second example. These healthy negative emotions, although uncomfortable, are less painful.

Can you see how telling yourself things like those in the first example churns you up? That you are feeding your feelings with thoughts that would greatly upset anyone who was being abused? And of course unhealthy feelings lead to unhealthy behavior.

PREFERENCES ARE SELF-HELPING
DEMANDS ARE SELF-SABOTAGING

According to REBT, an emotion is considered healthy when it serves your goals, desires, and values. It is unhealthy when it does not. Presumably your main goal is to stay alive and be happy—especially in your relationship with your partner. This can best be achieved by choosing to *prefer* rather than to *demand* that things be different.

When you make a demand, you box yourself in. Demands are absolute and do not leave room for any alternatives. They insist that things be the way you want them to be and that nothing else will do. They assume you have the power to run the universe: "I *absolutely, positively should not* be verbally abused! It *must* stop immediately!" When a demand is blocked or frustrated, it leads to unhealthy negative feelings like anguish and rage.

A preference, even a strong one, does not box you in. Preferences are not absolute and do not assume that you have the power to run the universe. When a preference is blocked or frustrated it leads to healthy negative feelings of disappointment and annoyance, and it leaves you with alternatives that help you cope. It allows you to want something and to try to get it, without holding your breath and turning blue in the face until you do.

With a demand you want whatever you want the way you want it—and there are no *buts* about it. With a preference you want whatever you want—*but* you recognize that what is, is, and you leave yourself some room to work with it: "I don't like my partner's abuse, *but* he can still abuse me; *but* I may not be able to stop him; *but* I can always leave him; *but* it won't kill me; *but* I can be happy in spite of it."

Musts, demands, and absolutes are unhealthy and irrational because they

- Insist that your partner and the world be different than they are
- Encourage your abuser to make himself angrier at you and become more abusive
- Stir up strong emotions that prevent you from thinking of and using appropriate tactics to deal with your abuse
- Rip up your gut and sap the joy from your life

Your irrational beliefs about your being verbally abused will not stop the abuse and will very likely make you behave in ways that will encourage more of it. Ironically—and pitifully—it adds your abuse of yourself to that of your partner. Now both of you are persecuting you! That is the really sad thing.

But lets assume that, for whatever reasons, you have decided to stay with your abuser. However, just because you are staying, doesn't mean you want to continue feeling terribly upset about his verbal blows, and you *do* want to handle him and his abuse as best you can. REBT aids both of these strong desires and helps you stay intact.

As we have said before, you usually cannot stop your partner's abuse, but if you use REBT, you can almost always stop your *self*-abuse. For again, you do have a choice. You can choose to *wish* your abuser would stop—or you can *command* that he do so. Your rational wish, if not fulfilled, will lead you to healthy negative feelings of regret and disappointment—and to a better approach to your dealing with abuse. Your irrational demand, if not fulfilled, will lead you to unhealthy negative feelings of anguish and rage—and to an unproductive approach.

So you *choose* to rationally prefer rather than to irrationally demand. That's good. But exactly *how* can you do this? You will learn many specific ways in this book. Let's start with a very important one—disputing your irrational beliefs.

Why is disputing necessary? Because it won't work to just tell yourself, "Well, because musts and demands cause me a lot of trouble, I'll simply change them to preferences." Your demands, musts, and absolutes—both learned and invented—are quite natural to you. You have held them and practiced them for many years. Since you still strongly believe them, giving them up will not be easy. Old habits die hard. If you really want to feel better, you are going to have to convince yourself to do what it takes to really, deeply let go of them. That means learning how to dispute.

HOW TO DISPUTE YOUR SELF-SABOTAGING IRRATIONAL BELIEFS

A major cause of emotional distress and poor coping ability is that your thoughts often reflect what you *believe* the facts of a particular situation to be, rather than what it *objectively is*. To be considered rational, beliefs have to be verifiable. As you learn to dispute your irrational thoughts and beliefs it may help to think of yourself as a detective, trying as best you can to find solid proof that backs up what you are telling yourself. When proof is lacking, convince yourself and finally accept that you don't have a viable, provable "case."

Another way to approach this is to think of yourself as a scientist, searching for verifiable proof that your theory—your belief—is fact and your logic is valid. This process, too, will help you examine and revise your old beliefs so they work *for* you, rather than a*gainst* you. Once you have questioned the truth and logic of your belief, it is important to also question the results you are getting by holding on to it.

How do you go about disputing? Simply by arguing with the "voice in your head" that is making the irrational statements—statements that cause your extreme, unhealthy negative emotions. REBT teaches you to dispute by asking yourself questions that challenge your irrational thoughts and beliefs, then to challenge the advisability of holding on to them, and finally to replace them with rational ones.

Let's see how this process worked for Susan. One day her husband, Jim, made his usual crazy-making remarks and then went off to work. Susan was so upset she could hardly concentrate on what she was doing. Later, she realized that her anguish and rage had been growing all day—and her abusive husband wasn't even there. She remembered what she had learned from REBT: Her thoughts were creating her emotions. She paid attention to the thoughts that were going through her mind, and she heard herself say, "Jim absolutely *must* stop abusing me!" She recognized that her demanding *must*—not her husband—was responsible for her unhealthy negative emotions.

Susan knew the next step to making herself feel better was to dispute her irrational belief that Jim *had to* stop abusing her. So she asked herself: "Why *must* he? Where is it written? What law of the universe commands that he absolutely *must* stop?" Then she answered her questions: "Obviously there's no reason why he *has* to stop, though I really wish he would. The idea that he has to stop isn't written anywhere except in my head. There is no law of the universe that commands him to do that or anything else just because I want him to or just because it is wrong."

Once she realized that she couldn't come up with any proof or evidence that what she had been telling herself was true, she went on to the next step. Susan thought about what she would get out of continuing to say that Jim absolutely must stop abusing her. She asked herself two important questions: "Does telling myself that Jim absolutely must stop abusing me get me what I want?" and "Does it help me feel the way I want to feel?" She knew the answers immediately: "Obviously it doesn't do either one, because I have been thinking this way for a long time, and it hasn't stopped Jim's abuse or made me feel any better. In fact, saying this stuff to myself all the time has made me feel much, much worse."

Susan came to this conclusion: "Because I now see that what I have been telling myself isn't true, doesn't get me what I want, and makes me extremely upset, I'm not going to say it anymore. Instead, I'm going to start telling myself "I would *prefer* that Jim stop abusing me, *but* it isn't the end of the world if he doesn't."

Susan realized that choosing to use a preference instead of making a demand gave her options. She knew she would still very much dislike Jim's abuse, *but* that it won't kill her, *but* that she can choose to be happy in spite of it, *but* that she can always leave him." This became Susan's new philosophy. It made her feel much better, and she knew that the next time Jim became abusive she would not feel as upset.

When Susan thought back to the REBT disputing steps she had used, she was surprised at how easily she had been able to

- Become aware that she was upset
- Remember that her upset feelings were being caused by what she was thinking
- Pay attention to what she was thinking
- Use questions to challenge the truth of what she was telling herself
- Conclude that what she was thinking was untrue, unprovable, hadn't stopped Jim's abuse, and was making her extremely upset

- Choose to let go of her old irrational demanding thought and replace it with a new rational preference
- Turn her new rational preference into an effective new philosophy that would reduce her pain and improve her life

You can learn how to do what Susan did. You can teach yourself to recognize what you're thinking that is making you upset. You can use disputing questions to examine what you are telling yourself and to help you decide if it makes sense to continue saying it. And you can learn how to answer the questions in a way that will change your thinking and make you feel better. So let's get started.

A Simple Formula for Using Disputing Questions

In REBT there are three main categories of disputing questions. Each category attacks irrational thoughts and beliefs from a different perspective.

#1: Questions the truth or logic of the belief
#2: Asks for proof or evidence that the belief is true
#3: Asks what results you will get if you continue to hold on to your old irrational belief

To question the truth or logic of a thought or belief (category 1), ask yourself such questions as: Is that true? How do I know? Is it logical? Why? How does it follow?

To ask for proof or evidence that the thought or belief is true (category 2), ask such questions as: Where is the proof? Where is the evidence? Where is it written? What law of the universe commands it?

To question the results you will get if you hold on to the thought or belief (category 3), ask such questions as: What results will I get if I continue to believe this? Does this thought get me what I want? Does it help me feel the way I want to feel?

The first two categories of disputing questions often overlap. Don't be concerned about which category a particular question falls into. When you are doing your own disputing, simply ask whichever questions seem to fit the irrational thought or belief you are working on at the time.

After asking questions from the first or second category or both, always ask questions from the third: What results will I get if I continue to hold on to my old irrational belief?

The answers to these questions will lead to your concluding that it would be wise to give up your old irrational way of thinking and see things in a new way. As we said previously, in REBT this new way of seeing things is called an effective new philosophy.

Using Disputing to Establish an Effective New Philosophy

Remember, the goal of disputing your irrational thoughts and beliefs (point D in the ABCs of Emotions, page 73) is to arrive at an effective new philosophy (point E) that will result in changing your unhealthy negative emotions into healthy negative ones.

Reading over the following examples several times will train your mind in a new way of thinking. Notice that the questions vary when we ask the first two types of disputing questions. However, when we talk about results, the question, answer, and conclusion are worded the same. Why? Because irrational thoughts generally lead to similar poor results. When you do your own disputing, you can vary the wording.

Once you review the two examples below and those in the following chapter, you will find it easy to ask and quickly answer disputing questions about your own irrational beliefs, just as Susan did. It may look complicated on paper, but once you get the idea, it's fast, easy to do, and can even be fun.

(Old) Irrational Belief: "My partner absolutely *must* stop abusing me!"

Disputing (category 1 or 2 or both): "Why *must* he?" "Where is it written?" "What law of the universe commands that he absolutely *must* stop?"

Answer (Effective New Philosophy): "Obviously there's no reason why he *has* to stop, though it would be highly preferable if he did. The idea that he has to stop is not written anywhere except in my head. It's hardly a law of the universe—but only a social and moral rule that he obviously is not following."

Disputing (category 3): "What results will I get if I continue to hold on to my old irrational belief?" "Does this thought get me what I want?" "Does it help me feel the way I want to feel?"

Answer (Effective New Philosophy): "Continuing to hold on to my old irrational belief won't change my partner or make him stop abusing me. It won't change me or help me stop abusing myself, either. It will only lead to more frustration, anger, and pain. I will be fighting an internal battle that cannot be won. It will never get me what I want or help me feel the way I want to feel."

Conclusion: "Because I now see that my old irrational belief is untrue and illogical, won't get me what I want, and is destructive to me, I will let go of it and replace it with a new rational belief."

(New) Rational Belief: "Although I strongly dislike my partner's verbal abuse and would *prefer* that he stop it, it isn't the end of the world if he doesn't."

Notice that each time you finish effectively disputing one of your old irrational beliefs, you will have reached the conclusion that you have to let go of it because it is untrue, illogical, and unprovable, and it won't get you what you want or help you feel the way you want to feel. Then you will replace it with a new rational belief that states a preference, rather than a must, should, ought, or demand. See how this works in the next example.

(Old) Irrational Belief: "He *can't* treat me this way!"

Disputing (category 1 or 2 or both): "Is that true?" "Is it logical?"

Answer (Effective New Philosophy): "No, it's not logical to keep telling myself that he can't treat me this way when he obviously is. I'd better face the fact that as unacceptable as his behavior is, and as much as it goes against moral and social rules, he is doing it anyway—but that doesn't mean I have to upset myself over it. And I always have the choice to leave him."

Disputing (category 3): "What results will I get if I continue to hold on to my old irrational belief?" "Does this thought get me what I want?" "Does it help me feel the way I want to feel?"

Answer (Effective New Philosophy): "Continuing to hold

on to my old irrational belief won't change my partner and make him stop abusing me. It won't change me or help me stop abusing myself, either. It will only lead to more frustration, anger, and pain. I will be fighting an internal battle that cannot be won. It will never get me what I want or help me feel the way I want to feel."

Conclusion: "Because I now see that my old irrational belief is untrue and illogical, won't get me what I want, and is destructive to me, I will let go of it and replace it with a new rational belief."

(New) Rational Belief: "Although my partner is treating me badly, and I would be much happier if he would treat me nicely, I don't have to get myself all upset over it."

HOW TO AVOID DISPUTING INEFFECTIVELY

Does disputing your irrational beliefs and coming up with effective new philosophies always help? Almost always, but you do need to be careful to avoid the pitfalls.

A common mistake is using your wants, feelings, and opinions as "proof" that your irrational belief is valid.

Irrational Belief: "My partner absolutely *must* stop verbally abusing me!"

Disputing: "Why *must* he stop?"

Incorrect Answers: "Because I don't want it to happen anymore." "Because I hate it." "Because it's wrong."

Correct Answer (Effective New Philosophy): "Obviously there's no reason why he *has* to stop, though I would really *prefer* that he do so."

Another common mistake is disputing your irrational beliefs properly, arriving at the right answers, but still not really believing and feeling them. For example, you can ask yourself "Why must my abuser stop abusing me?" and correctly answer, "Obviously, he doesn't *have* to stop—because he doesn't. Too bad! But that's the way it is." However, underneath this correct answer to your self-questioning, which you only *lightly* believe, you can still *strongly* believe, "I don't care! Because he is so wrong, he *must* stop!"

Don't worry if this happens. You are learning a new way of

thinking and talking to yourself, and it can take time for the emotions to catch up to the intellect. Be patient and keep working at convincing yourself of the rational, logical truth. Keep challenging and disputing. Eventually the truth will sink in. REBT emotive and behavioral methods, which you will learn in later chapters, will also help speed up this acceptance process. Remember that millions of people just like you have learned to dispute effectively.

WHAT TO DO AS SOON AS YOU BEGIN TO FEEL UPSET

As we have said, before you can stop doing anything, you first have to realize that you are *doing* it. Next, you have to see *how* you are doing it. Then you have to *stop* doing it. As you read in the last chapter, sometimes just knowing that you are upsetting yourself with your thoughts will be enough for you to stop. Other times it will be necessary to have specific steps in mind. Here is a checklist of those you learned in this chapter:

1. Become aware that you are getting upset.
2. Remind yourself that you are getting upset because of what you are telling yourself.
3. Listen to what you are telling yourself.
4. Remind yourself that to reduce your feelings of being upset you need to change the extreme, self-sabotaging statements you are making to yourself to more moderate, self-helping ones.
5. Use your disputing technique to question what you are telling yourself. Ask such questions as: Is it true? Is it logical? Why? Where is the proof? What results will I get if I continue to believe this?
6. Recognize that what you are telling yourself is unprovable, illogical, isn't working, and is causing you great emotional pain.
7. Change your extreme, self-sabotaging statements to more moderate, self-helping ones.

Little by little these steps will become familiar and easy to use, but it is a process that may take time. At first you probably will not realize you have upset yourself with your irrational thinking until after you have done it. Soon you will realize you are upsetting yourself while you are still doing it. Then you will realize you are beginning to upset yourself when you first begin to think irrationally, and you will be able to stop it before you become upset. Eventually, thinking more rationally in the first place will become second nature to you.

The disputing technique you have just learned can be used with many other kinds of destructive thinking. In chapter 9, we describe some of these other thinking habits and use examples to teach you how to put a stop to them.

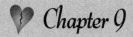

Stopping the Thinking That Does You In

Now you know that your old way of thinking will not make your situation better, make your partner understand, or stop your pain. And you have seen how disputing will teach you a new way of thinking that will make a difference.

Let's briefly review what happens when you dispute. You begin with an old irrational belief, think it through, and then replace it with a new rational belief. This is good, clear, unemotional straight thinking. Now we will use the old irrational belief that we disputed in the last chapter to see what your new rational straight thinking looks like.

NEW RATIONAL STRAIGHT THINKING

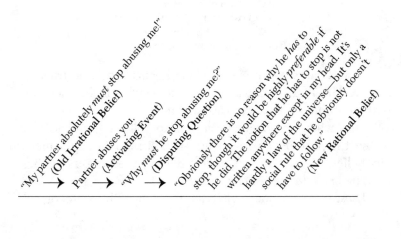

"My partner absolutely *must* stop abusing me!" (Old Irrational Belief) → Partner abuses you. (Activating Event) → "Why *must* he stop abusing me?" (Disputing Question) → "Obviously there is no reason why he *has to* stop, though it would be highly *preferable* if he did. The notion that he has to stop is not written anywhere except in my head. It's hardly a law of the universe—but only a social rule that he obviously doesn't have to follow." (New Rational Belief)

The old way of thinking you have been using, the kind that has gotten you into so much trouble, is very different. It is muddled, emotional circular thinking. When you use this kind of thinking, you begin with an old irrational belief, think it through, and end up right back where you started, with the same old irrational belief. The only thing you accomplish is that you manage to upset yourself, and then to upset yourself even more. Now let's use the same old irrational belief we just talked about to see what circular thinking looks like.

OLD IRRATIONAL CIRCULAR THINKING

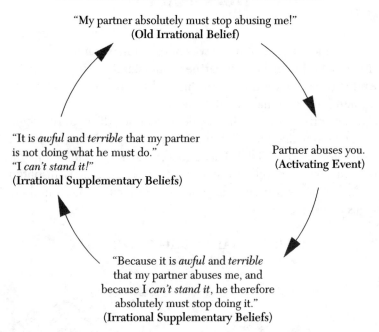

"My partner absolutely must stop abusing me!"
(Old Irrational Belief)

Partner abuses you.
(Activating Event)

"Because it is *awful* and *terrible* that my partner abuses me, and because I *can't stand it*, he therefore absolutely must stop doing it."
(Irrational Supplementary Beliefs)

"It is *awful* and *terrible* that my partner is not doing what he must do."
"I *can't stand it!*"
(Irrational Supplementary Beliefs)

As you can see, circular thinking begins with a destructive irrational belief that states a must, should, ought, or demand: "My partner absolutely *must* stop abusing me!"

Then when your dogmatic *must* is not followed, you move to the next step. Your irrational belief gives birth to the supplementary beliefs "It is *awful* and *terrible* that my partner is not doing what he *must* do" and "I *can't stand it!*"

These supplementary beliefs tend to "prove" that your original dogmatic *must* is true—and often lead to still more dogmatic demands. Without stopping to question these beliefs, you may then conclude: "Because it is *awful* and *terrible* that my partner abuses me, and because I *can't stand it,* he therefore absolutely *must* stop doing it!"

Notice how these irrational supplementary beliefs cycle back to the original irrational belief "My partner absolutely *must* stop abusing me!" Circular thinking becomes automatic and strongly reinforces your irrational awfulizing, terribilizing, *must*uabatory, and I-can't-stand-it beliefs, making you more dogmatic and absolutistic than ever. These thoughts all go around and around in your head, firing up your emotions—*making* you upset and *keeping* you upset.

The way to feel better is to move from your initial automatic irrational pain-*producing* thought to a new rational pain-*reducing* thought. That is exactly what disputing helps you do.

HOW TO CHANGE YOUR OLD IRRATIONAL CIRCULAR THINKING TO NEW RATIONAL STRAIGHT THINKING

We will now go over in detail the two supplementary beliefs used in our old irrational circular thinking example and show you how to change them to new rational straight thinking by actively and vigorously disputing them.

Some of the following material may make it may seem as if we are not taking the severity of your abuse seriously. Be assured that we are. However, the *more* you tell yourself how horrible the abuse is, the *worse* you will feel. The *less* you tell yourself how horrible the abuse is, the *better* you will feel. To achieve your goal of feeling better, you need to learn how to step back from a highly emotional situation long enough to see it through new rational eyes. So keep an open mind and try to gain some perspective on what is happening. If you continue to see your abuse through overly emotional eyes, the result will be extreme negative thoughts that are guaranteed to keep you in pain.

Awfulizing and Terribilizing

As you now know, when you use certain words they tend to inflame you and create powerful negative emotions. This is particularly true of *awful* and *terrible* and similar words. These words are almost always an unrealistic exaggeration. It's not the words themselves that cause problems but the attitude behind them. As soon as you label something awful or terrible, it becomes much worse than it has to be.

If you tell yourself that being verbally abused is very bad, you are right, because it goes against one of your main goals in life: to have your partner treat you fairly, kindly, and lovingly. But if you tell yourself that it is *awful* and *terrible*, you are implying that it is so bad that it's worse than bad and that it *should not* and *must not* happen. Awfulizing beliefs sound very accurate, and you can easily convince yourself of them. Holding on to them, though, is wrong for two main reasons. First, they are not proven facts. Second, they keep you stuck in your pain.

No matter how *bad* being abused makes you feel, it is important to recognize and accept that it is *still* not *awful* and *terrible*. Saying that it is, elevates a very bad thing into a major catastrophe. If you really think about it, you will realize that there are worse things than being verbally abused. When you use words like *awful* and *terrible* to talk to yourself about your abuse, you create more negative feelings and make yourself feel worse. Then you are so focused on your pain you can't cope with what is going on or think of anything to do about it. You can dispute these exaggerated statements and concepts and change them as follows:

(Old) Irrational Belief: "It's *awful* and *terrible* that my partner is not doing what he *must* do—stop abusing me."

Disputing: "Where is the proof that it is *awful* and *terrible* that he is not doing what he *must* do?"

Answer (Effective New Philosophy): "There is no proof that it is awful and terrible. Just because I think it is, doesn't make it so. If I say that it is *awful* and *terrible* I am implying that it is so bad that it's worse than bad and that it *should not* and *must not* happen. But it *is* happening. And saying that it is awful and terrible only inflames me and makes things much worse than they have to be.

No matter how *bad* being abused makes me feel, I will recognize and accept that it is *still* not *awful* and *terrible*. Saying that it is, elevates a very bad thing into a major catastrophe. When I do this I am so focused on my pain that I can't cope with what is going on or think of anything to do about it. Although I would very much *prefer* that my partner stop abusing me, I will face the fact that things are as they are and that my demanding they be different will not change them. Not labeling anything awful or terrible will help me deal with my situation better.

Disputing: "What results will I get if I continue to hold on to my old irrational belief?" "Does this thought get me what I want?" "Does it help me feel the way I want to feel?"

Answer (Effective New Philosophy): "Continuing to hold on to my old irrational belief won't change my partner or make him stop abusing me. It won't change me or help me stop abusing myself, either. It will only lead to more frustration, anger, and pain. I will be fighting an internal battle that cannot be won. It will never get me what I want or help me feel the way I want to feel."

Conclusion: "Because I now see that my old irrational belief is untrue and illogical, won't get me what I want, and is destructive to me, I will let go of it and replace it with a new rational belief."

(New) Rational Belief: "Although my partner's abusing me is very *bad*, and I *prefer* that it not happen, I will not upset myself and turn it into a major catastrophe by saying that it is *awful* or *terrible*."

If you do this kind of REBT disputing after you have labeled your being verbally abused as awful and terrible, you will be able to give up thinking of your abuse in such an extreme way. You will no longer be stirring yourself up all the time. Your abuse will no longer be all you think about—and all you feel! You will still keep seeing your abuse as very bad but will no longer be seriously upset about it, and you will be able to cope with it better.

I-Can't-Stand-It-Itis

You, like many other people, may convince yourself that because you are being verbally abused by your partner, which absolutely *should not* and *must not* occur, you *can't stand it*—cannot tolerate it at all. This is almost always a false self-statement, because if you *really* can't stand something, cannot tolerate it at all, you will probably die if it occurs. Or, if the thing you *can't stand* happens and you don't die, you couldn't possibly have *any* pleasure or joy *at all* in life. You can dispute these highly exaggerated notions as follows:

(Old) Irrational Beliefs: "Because my partner absolutely *must* stop abusing me, I *can't stand it* when he still does it. And I will *never* be able to have *any* pleasure or joy in life as long as he continues to abuse me."

Disputing: "I'll always intensely dislike my partner's verbally abusing me, but why can't I stand it?" "Will I die from it?"

Answer (Effective New Philosophy): "No, I definitely can stand it in the sense that I will not die from it, unless I continue to greatly upset myself about it. Then I might make myself so sick that I could die or be driven to commit suicide, and these I can avoid doing."

Disputing: "My partner's verbal abuse is highly obnoxious and uncalled for." "But is it true that I cannot have any pleasure or joy in life at all if he doesn't stop abusing me?"

Answer (Effective New Philosophy): "No, it isn't true. I am not in an all-or-nothing situation. If I insist on staying with him despite his abuse, I will have less pleasure and joy than I would have if he were not abusive, but that doesn't mean I won't have any. If I force myself to stop focusing on my being abused, and start focusing on making my life more pleasurable and enjoyable, I can figure out ways to do it—with other people, with new interests, and perhaps even with my partner at times. It is not inevitable that I live a pleasureless, joyless life."

Disputing: "What results will I get if I continue to hold on to my old irrational belief?" "Does this thought get me what I want?" "Does it help me feel the way I want to feel?"

Answer (Effective New Philosophy): "Continuing to hold on to my old irrational belief won't change my partner or make him stop abusing me. It won't change me or help me stop abusing myself, either. It will only lead to more frustration, anger, and pain. I will be fighting an internal battle that cannot be won. It will never get me what I want or help me feel the way I want to feel."

Conclusion: "Because I now see that my old irrational belief is untrue and illogical, won't get me what I want, and is destructive to me, I will let go of it and replace it with a new rational belief."

(New) Rational Belief: Come up with a new rational belief yourself this time. Remember that it is generally a restatement of the old irrational belief, using a healthy self-helping preference rather than an unhealthy self-sabotaging must, should, ought, or demand. It reflects the rational truth you have learned by disputing. (For help, see the previous example in this chapter and the examples in chapter 8.)

CONQUERING OTHER MAJOR THOUGHT PATTERNS THAT MAKE YOU FEEL CRAZY

As you have learned, even though your abusive partner's behavior is what it is, your own irrational thinking is what causes most of your pain. The automatic circular thinking we have been talking about is one kind of irrational thinking that can cause you problems. Other distorted thought patterns can also keep you feeling extremely upset and out of control.

(I [A.E.] was one of the first authorities to use categories of distorted thought patterns. I originated many and wrote about them in my numerous articles and books about REBT. Aaron Beck, Donald Meichenbaum, David Burns, and other authorities on cognitive behavior therapy added more categories. These thought patterns became widely known and are commonly used today.)

Once you are able to put your irrational thinking into one or more of these categories, you will be better able to deal with the irrational beliefs they foster. Here are some common irrational thought patterns and examples of quick and forceful disputing that will help you stop thinking in these destructive ways.

Obsessing

How often have you found yourself thinking about a recent abusive incident, replaying it word for word in your mind, analyzing and reanalyzing it, trying to figure out what really happened and what your part in it might have been? Each time you do this the words spin around and around in your mind as you keep trying to make sense of it all. If only you could understand. If only you could make your partner understand. If only you could get him to stop treating you as he does.

Time and again your precious mental energy is sapped as you struggle with each abusive incident and each issue that comes up. Often, no matter where you are and what is going on around you, you feel as though you are alone in a world of your own thoughts. You desperately want to stop the crazy-making talk from racing around in your head, but you can't get rid of it.

Obsessing comes as naturally as breathing. Do you remember learning as a child that if you have a problem, you have only to think it through, and if necessary, to think it through again and again, until you come up with a workable solution? You have practiced this kind of thinking thousands of times from early childhood. Therefore, when you are upset about being verbally abused, you try to resolve the problem by resorting to the type of thinking you know best, but it is one of the most destructive things abused partners do to themselves.

How can you stop obsessing? There are a variety of widely known practical methods, from repeatedly saying "Stop!" and visualizing a big red stop sign to snapping a rubber band worn on your wrist; from writing down your thoughts to doing something that requires a lot of concentration. Although these can be helpful, our primary concern here is getting to the *cause* of your tendency to obsess about your abuse in the first place. So let's look at a basic irrational belief that can cause you to go over and over the same thing in your mind, making you feel anxious and out of control.

(Old) Irrational Belief: "Because being verbally abused by my partner is so incredibly bad, and because it *absolutely must not* happen, I *have to* keep thinking about it all the time until I find a way to stop it!"

Disputing: "Why must I keep thinking about this bad thing all the time?" "I want to think of a way to stop the abuse, but does that prove I *have to* do so?" "Does it follow that my constantly thinking about it will help me find a way to stop it?" "Will it do any good at all?"

Answer (Effective New Philosophy): "I don't have to keep thinking about this bad thing. In fact, I now know that even if I were to think my obsessive thoughts until the end of time, it would not change one thing about my abusive partner's behavior. Figuring out whether or not there is a shred of truth to something he said about the way I *am* or about what I *did* isn't the answer either. It doesn't matter because he would still be abusing me even if I were perfect. Obviously, my obsessing about this verbal abuse won't help me find a way to stop it. In fact, my constantly thinking about it will disrupt my life and do much more harm than good. It's an old habit that I can break."

Disputing: "What results will I get if I continue to hold on to my old irrational belief?" "Does this thought get me what I want?" "Does it help me feel the way I want to feel?"

Answer (Effective New Philosophy): "Continuing to hold on to my old irrational belief won't change my partner or make him stop abusing me. It won't change me or help me stop abusing myself, either. It will only lead to more frustration, anger, and pain. I will be fighting an internal battle that cannot be won. It will never get me what I want or help me feel the way I want to feel."

Conclusion: It's your turn to come to a rational conclusion that states your decision to let go of your old belief and gives reasons why it makes sense to do so. You can use our wording from previous examples or you can use your own words.

(New) Rational Belief: Now state your new rational belief.

Emotional Reasoning

When you get caught up in your emotions, it is all too easy to lose sight of what is really going on in your life. You no longer trust your perceptions because your partner has repeatedly challenged them, and you have allowed yourself to get into the habit of accepting his perceptions over your own.

Although it seems natural to rely on your emotions to help tell you what is going on, they too have become unreliable because they have been so battered. One minute you are able to see the particulars of an abusive situation clearly; the next minute everything becomes gray and foggy, and you are unsure of what has just happened. You feel confused, insecure, and out of control. When emotions are flooding your mind, logic and reason are pushed aside. In this state it is easy to assume that your negative emotions reflect the way things really are: "I feel it, therefore it must be true."

(Old) Irrational Beliefs: "Because I can't stop feeling overwhelmed by my emotions when I am being abused, and I know that I *must* do so, I feel helpless. My strong feeling that I am helpless proves that I really am!"

Disputing: "How does my strong feeling that I am helpless prove that I really am?"

Answer (Effective New Philosophy): "My feeling of helplessness when I'm overwhelmed by my emotions only proves that I have that feeling. Just because I *feel* helpless doesn't mean that I *am*. My feelings do not provide verifiable evidence that my belief is true. I cause myself great pain when I use my emotions as proof instead of using reason and logic. I now know that I can use REBT techniques to keep myself from becoming overwhelmed by my emotions when I am being abused. I am not helpless!"

Disputing: "What results will I get if I continue to hold on to my old irrational belief?" "Does this thought get me what I want?" "Does it help me feel the way I want to feel?"

Answer (Effective New Philosophy): "Continuing to hold on to my old irrational belief won't change my partner or make him stop abusing me. It won't change me or help me stop abusing myself, either. It will only lead to more frustration, anger, and pain. I will be fighting an internal battle that cannot be won. It will never get me what I want or help me feel the way I want to feel."

Conclusion: Arrive at a conclusion.

(New) Rational Belief: Here is another opportunity to practice stating a new rational belief.

Personalizing

Abuse seems very personal. After all, it is directed right at you. But personalizing in the sense that we are talking about here means that you see yourself as the cause of your abusive partner's anger, even though you are not primarily responsible for it. He breaks you down by repeated attacks until you no longer know who you are. Then you take his word that your weaknesses and mistakes are responsible for his anger and that you deserve the abuse you are receiving. Because your partner's verbal bullets hit you in your most vulnerable spots, you become confused and unable to tell whether what he says is true. You at least partly accept his blame, and you blame yourself for *being* as you are and for *doing* as you do.

(Old) Irrational Belief: "Because my partner keeps verbally abusing me, and because he does so frequently and is so positive that he is right, he must *be* right about my having these faults and about my being to blame for the abuse and for the bad things that happen."

Disputing: "Does it necessarily follow that because my partner says I have certain faults, that I have them?" "And even if I do have some of the faults he accuses me of having, does it necessarily mean that I am responsible for his anger and abuse?"

Answer (Effective New Philosophy): "It doesn't necessarily follow that because my partner says I have certain faults, that I have them. I now know that he will do or say anything to vent his old pent-up anger and to try to control me. Therefore I cannot trust that what he says is true. And even if I do have some of these faults, it does not make me responsible for his anger or his abuse. Even if he were with a different partner, he would be abusive. So although it feels like a personal attack when I am verbally abused, I must remind myself again and again that the abuse is not about me or anything I say or anything I do."

Disputing: "What results will I get if I continue to hold on to my old irrational belief?" "Does this thought get me what I want?" "Does it help me feel the way I want to feel?"

Answer (Effective New Philosophy): "Continuing to hold on to my old irrational belief won't change my partner or make him stop abusing me. It won't change me or help me stop abusing myself, either. It will only lead to more frustration, anger, and pain. I will be fighting an internal battle that cannot be won. It will never get me what I want or help me feel the way I want to feel."

Conclusion: Arrive at a conclusion.

(New) Rational Belief: State a new rational belief. (Isn't it getting easier?)

Overgeneralizing

When you overgeneralize, you see a single negative event or series of events as a never-ending pattern of defeat. "Sometimes" becomes "always," "seldom" becomes "never," "some" becomes "all," and "temporary" becomes "forever." You may tend to generalize about a variety of issues in your relationships and in your life. You can dispute inaccurate overgeneralizations as follows:

(Old) Irrational Belief: "Because I have not been coping well with my partner's verbal abuse, I will *never* be able to cope with it. I can never in any way cope satisfactorily with abuse, either to change it or to change my supercharged reactions to it. My life will always be this way."

Disputing: "It's true I have not been coping well with my partner's verbal abuse, and have not been effective in trying to change it or to change my supercharged reactions to it, but how does this show that I will never learn to do better?"

Answer (Effective New Philosophy): "It doesn't. I may not be able to change the fact that I am being abused, but my coping poorly with it merely shows that I have not yet learned to cope better, not that I can't learn. I'm on the right track now. I'm developing new thinking skills, and if I stop seriously upsetting myself about my partner's behavior, I will give myself a much better chance of coping effectively with it. My coping better will change the interaction between us, and the quality of my life can improve."

Disputing: "What results will I get if I continue to hold on to my old irrational belief?" "Does this thought get me what I want?"

"Does it help me feel the way I want to feel?"

Answer (Effective New Philosophy): "Continuing to hold on to my old irrational belief won't change my partner or make him stop abusing me. It won't change me or help me stop abusing myself, either. It will only lead to more frustration, anger, and pain. I will be fighting an internal battle that cannot be won. It will never get me what I want or help me feel the way I want to feel."

Conclusion: Arrive at a conclusion.

(New) Rational Belief: State a new rational belief.

Magnifying and Minimizing

As illogical as it may sound, you probably vacillate between magnifying and minimizing your partner's abusive behavior. Most abused partners do. When he is being mean, his meanness looms larger than life (magnifying). When he is being nice again, it doesn't seem as if the bad times were so bad or all that important (minimizing). In fact, once an abusive incident is over, you may not clearly remember how hurt you felt or exactly what happened. This flip-flopping from magnifying to minimizing your partner's abusive behavior keeps you off balance and out of touch with the truth of your situation.

You may also magnify his nice behavior. You may be so hungry for love and affection that even when your partner is tossing you "crumbs of niceness," you perceive his behavior as wonderful. Magnifying nice behavior can keep you hooked into the relationship more than ever. "After all," you say to yourself, "the good times are soooo good! Who in their right mind would consider leaving?" You have a glimmer of hope that he might change and become nice all the time.

You may also magnify some aspects of your own behavior and minimize others—magnify your shortcomings and mistakes, and minimize your good qualities and abilities. You are magnifying if when you do one little thing you think you shouldn't have done, you blow it out of proportion, as if you were posting it on a scoreboard at the sports arena. You are minimizing when you don't give yourself enough credit for who you are and what you are capable of doing.

(Old) Irrational Belief (Magnifying): "Making that mistake was so embarrassing. And now that my partner has nastily pointed it out in front of everyone, I'll never live it down. Everyone will think I'm stupid and will always remember my blunder. This has ruined my life!"

Disputing: "How does it follow that just because I made a mistake, I am stupid?" "What proof is there that everyone is thinking about what I did and will never forget it?"

Answer (Effective New Philosophy): "It doesn't follow that because I made a mistake I am stupid. Everyone makes mistakes. What I *do* is not who I *am*. And there is no proof that the other people gave my mistake more than a moment's thought. They certainly aren't thinking about it anymore. I'm the only one who's dwelling on it, making it bigger than life. The fact that my partner nastily pointed it out in front of other people is a reflection on him, not me. It's important for me to recognize that my mistakes take on gigantic proportions because I am unsure of myself, and because I am in the habit of focusing on my negative points and discounting my positive ones. I must become aware of the times I am exaggerating my faults and mistakes, so that I can stop doing it. I will also give myself more credit for the things I do well, which will make me less vulnerable to feeling stupid."

Disputing: "What results will I get if I continue to hold on to my old irrational belief?" "Does this thought get me what I want?" "Does it help me feel the way I want to feel?"

Answer (Effective New Philosophy): "Continuing to hold on to my old irrational belief won't change my partner or make him stop abusing me. It won't change me or help me stop abusing myself, either. It will only lead to more frustration, anger, and pain. I will be fighting an internal battle that cannot be won. It will never get me what I want or help me feel the way I want to feel."

Conclusion: Arrive at a conclusion.

(New) Rational Belief: State a new rational belief.

(Old) Irrational Belief (Minimizing): "Because my partner is so much nicer to me today, he probably didn't mean the things he said last night. Maybe it wasn't as bad as I thought. I can hardly remember exactly what happened anyway. Maybe everything is going to be better from now on."

Disputing: "Does it necessarily follow that because my partner is nicer today, that he didn't mean the things he said last night or that they weren't as bad as I thought?" "Because I can hardly remember what happened, does that mean that what he said was no big deal?" "Because he is nicer today, does that prove that he will continue to be nice in the future?"

Answer (Effective New Philosophy): "Just because my partner is nicer to me today, it doesn't follow that he didn't mean the things he said last night. And just because I can hardly remember how bad it was doesn't prove it wasn't bad. I need to remind myself that switching from a Dr. Jekyll to a Mr. Hyde and back again is part of the abusive cycle. And forgetting parts of painful experiences is one way my mind tries to protect me. It is important to acknowledge that I was treated abusively, without either exaggerating or minimizing it. This is the only way I will be able to make rational decisions about how to cope with the abuse and what to do with my life. Denial is my enemy. I will fight it."

Disputing: "What results will I get if I continue to hold on to my old irrational belief?" "Does this thought get me what I want?" "Does it help me feel the way I want to feel?"

Answer (Effective New Philosophy): "Continuing to hold on to my old irrational belief won't change my partner or make him stop abusing me. It won't change me or help me stop abusing myself, either. It will only lead to more frustration, anger, and pain. I will be fighting an internal battle that cannot be won. It will never get me what I want or help me feel the way I want to feel."

Conclusion: Arrive at a conclusion.

(New) Rational Belief: State a new rational belief.

Thinking Perfectionistically

Almost everyone has heard about perfectionism and knows how destructive it is. Some people set impossible standards for themselves, strive to achieve them, and then beat themselves up when they can't live up to them. Perfectionism is particularly destructive to those in abusive relationships, many of whom think that if they could only be perfect enough their partner would love them and have no reason to abuse them. But no matter how perfect they drive themselves to become, it only compounds their problems. It sets them up to fail, to endlessly question their part in the abuse, and to hate themselves.

(Old) Irrational Beliefs: "I *must not* have any serious faults or make any mistakes that my partner can abuse me about. I have to be perfect, so that I will know once and for all that the abuse is not my fault."

Disputing: "Why *must* I not have any serious faults or make any mistakes that my partner can abuse me about?" "Where is it written that I have to be perfect?"

Answer (Effective New Philosophy): "No matter how hard I try, I cannot be so perfect that my partner will never abuse me. I will always be a fallible human. He can make an issue of some of my imperfections and can wrongly abuse me about them— but he doesn't need a reason to abuse. Even if I were perfect, my partner would think up something to abuse me about. I will keep reminding myself that dumping on me is my partner's way of venting anger he has about other things that have nothing to do with me."

Disputing: "What results will I get if I continue to hold on to my old irrational belief?" "Does this thought get me what I want?" "Does it help me feel the way I want to feel?"

Answer (Effective New Philosophy): "Continuing to hold on to my old irrational belief won't change my partner or make him stop abusing me. It won't change me or help me stop abusing myself, either. It will only lead to more frustration, anger, and pain. I will be fighting an internal battle that cannot be won. It will never get me what I want or help me feel the way I want to feel."

Conclusion: Arrive at a conclusion.
(New) Rational Belief: State a new rational belief.

You have learned the mechanics of disputing and read examples of how it works. You understand how to use disputing to change your destructive thinking, and therefore your destructive emotions. With practice, you will be able to focus on your upsetting thoughts and change them even in the midst of an abusive incident. Before you know it, you will quite naturally slip into a rational mode of thinking, no matter what is going on around you. (And in chapter 11 you will learn how to do shortcut disputing, which makes the process faster and easier.)

Your new thinking mode will put you on the road to self-empowerment. This road, however, must be built on a solid foundation of positive feelings about yourself, or it will repeatedly cave in. Your negative feelings about yourself got you into your present situation, and they continue to harm you by undermining your efforts to take back your personal power.

To ensure that your road to self-empowerment is solid and will support your efforts, you need to take a new look at yourself through accepting REBT eyes. The next chapter teaches you the REBT way to having healthy, more positive feelings about yourself.

Chapter 10

Getting Your Feelings About Yourself to Work *For*—Rather Than *Against*—You

Why do your partner's accusatory and discounting remarks so often reduce you to tears and trigger hours of obsessing? How can he get to you so easily? And why do his remarks cut so deep? Because they cut straight into the painful self-doubts and non-acceptance of yourself you have had since early childhood, setting off your tendency to blame yourself, feel guilty, and put yourself down. You deal with crisis after crisis, unaware that your insecurities are a big part of the problem. They compound your confusion and pain, and keep you from seeing how irrational your relationship is.

You damn yourself for being "the way you are" and for making mistakes, and you damn your partner for being "the way *he* is" and for what he is "doing to you." You make excuses for your partner's abusive behavior: "We're short of money." "He's pressured at work." "The kids were making too much noise." And you blame yourself: "I should have known." "I should have been more careful not to upset him." "If I were different, he might not act this way."

Even though you have learned from this book that you are not responsible for your partner's deplorable behavior, your insecurities about yourself can still make you vulnerable to "buying into" his accusations, believing his criticisms, and accepting that you should have somehow foreseen and prevented whatever upset him. When you think this way, you set yourself up for a double whammy—attacks by two abusers. You not only *allow* your partner to abuse you, you *help* him to abuse you—by abusing yourself. You help him plunge your *own* sword of non-acceptance of yourself deep into your heart. This non-acceptance creates a destructive pattern of thinking that causes you to react to your partner's hurtful remarks by blemishing your entire being and creating feelings of guilt, shame, worthlessness, anger, and depression. Understanding this cycle, and stopping it, is what this chapter is about.

WHY YOU PLAY YOUR PARTNER'S BLAME-SHAME GAME EVEN WHEN YOU KNOW BETTER

It would seem that once you have become aware of how abusive relationships work and understand that it is your partner's goal to make himself seem okay and you seem flawed and inferior, you would no longer be vulnerable to his abusive behavior. You would realize there is no basis for continuing your excruciating soul-searching, self-analysis, self-blame, and self-downing, since the abuse is not about *you*. His behavior would no longer cause you debilitating pain.

But does this knowledge actually stop the cycle of obsessive thoughts and out-of-control emotions? Not necessarily. It may be that you *still* get caught up in the old, familiar quagmire of confusion, pain, and tears—even when you know that your partner's behavior is irrational, that his statements about you are usually untrue, and that the abusive incidents are not your fault. Why? Because although you *know* better, a part of you gets caught up in what your partner says. A part of you thinks he may be right about you. A part of you still judges you harshly and sees you as lacking. A part of you believes that you may—as he insists—not be okay, after all. Insidiously, your insecurities, negative perception and non-acceptance of yourself, and your tendency to blame yourself and feel guilty set you up to play right into his hands.

Without a strong sense of self-worth and lovability, and a high level of self-acceptance, you will continue to be at the mercy of your partner's (and other people's) opinions of you. You will tend to judge yourself by his stringent criteria and see yourself through his angry eyes. As time after time he zeros in on your vulnerabilities, he will expertly bring out any insecurities or doubts you may have about yourself. He will relentlessly chip away at your already fragile self-image, self-worth, and self-respect. He will take advantage of your humanness and wound you in your soft spots. And the more wounded you become, the more easily injured you will be each time you are attacked—and the less able to cope.

As your partner hammers away at your inadequacies, you may come to believe more and more that you really *do* have them—and not only that you *have* them but also that it is *awful* to have them, and that they make you an *awful person*. And to your partner's condemnations you likely add your own, including blaming yourself for having gotten into your abusive relationship in the first place, and feeling guilty and weak for not being able to leave or to deal with it better.

The part of you that believes your partner may be right about you can push you deep into a vortex of doubt and confusion, self-blame and guilt, shame and self-hatred. As long as you share his non-acceptance and think his negative view of you could be partly true, you will continue to be deeply hurt by his abusive behavior. Perhaps even worse—you will continue to deeply hurt yourself by beating yourself up with cruel, critical self-talk long after his verbal attacks are over. And you will continue to be so entrapped by your habitual, painful mental gymnastics that you won't be able to think clearly enough to deal with his abuse.

HOW YOU PLAY THE BLAME-SHAME GAME

If you are like most abused partners, you agonize over whether there is any truth to your partner's accusations and criticisms. You believe the old adage that "it takes two" to cause problems, so you think you probably somehow play a part in creating the "problems" you are having. And being human, you likely have some doubts about yourself, which your abusive partner uses against you. The more self-doubts you have, the more critical of yourself you are, and the more you blame yourself and feel guilty and ashamed, the more effective your partner is at keeping you off-balance, confused, upset, and preoccupied with the things he says are "wrong" with you.

Although everyone finds dealing with abusive behavior a challenge, those who tend to judge themselves harshly and are prone to putting themselves down are more easily and more deeply hurt—in fact may feel wounded to their core—by an abusive partner's remarks. They are also quicker to feel shame, embarrassment, or humiliation.

If this is true of you, you probably can't let go of an abusive incident until you determine whether it is—even partly—a result of some fault, deficiency, or mistake of yours. You go over and over everything that was said, desperately trying to sort out fact from fiction. Could it be that you *were*—as your partner claims— careless or thoughtless, or that you *did* make the same mistake as before? After all, why would he say these things if they weren't true?

If you decide amidst your confusion that even a shred of what your partner said about you is true, you get caught up in a wave of self-blame, guilt, and shame for "being" as you are or having done as you did. You believe that perhaps he is right about you. Not only can't you do anything right, but apparently—as he frequently insists—your ability to remember "correctly" what has or has not taken place is faulty and unreliable, too. And at times, you may be convinced that he is right in blaming you for his anger and abusive behavior.

Even when you know—without a doubt—that the things your partner is saying about you are *not* true, you probably turn yourself inside out trying to "prove" to him that you are "innocent," and trying to make him understand that he is mistaken about you. That you are not "guilty," as charged. That you are okay after all. In fact, sometimes your life may seem to depend on "proving" it to him. Why do you go to such great lengths to prove your innocence? Because your feelings about yourself are dependent on your partner's feelings about you, and his opinion is crucial to your being able to feel good about yourself. You see yourself as he sees you.

Your partner's attacks may leave you confused and unsure of yourself. That's why whenever you *know* that what he is saying about you is wrong, you feel compelled to make him see it. If he can see that he is wrong *this* time, he may realize that he has been wrong *other* times. And then maybe he will see that you are not so bad after all—and you will be able to see yourself in a better light too.

Because you see yourself through your partner's eyes, shame, embarrassment, and humiliation rise up in you whether or not you have actually done anything wrong. These feelings do not stem from the wrongness of the act you are accused of, but from the bad view of your *self*, your whole *being*, you have when he thinks you did something wrong. Whether you really did anything wrong, or he just thinks you did, you not only agree that your *behavior* was bad, you tell yourself that your bad *behavior* makes *you* bad. Therefore, you have to somehow stop your accuser from thinking you acted shamefully.

But thinking you *are* what you *do* is ridiculous because you are a person who does millions of things—good, bad, and in between. Obviously you cannot judge your entire *being* based on any one of these acts. Even several of them cannot make you a *bad person*, since there are many more things you do that are not bad.

Your accuser, however, knows that you think you *are* what you *do*—that you judge your entire self based on your performance. He knows that you are a sucker for shame and that you will not merely feel sorry and disappointed if he can make you believe that you did something wrong, but that you will belabor yourself mercilessly. He may even put you down in front of others, knowing that you will take their disapproval of your acts as disapproval of *you*—and that you will agree with them.

HOW TO STOP PLAYING THE BLAME-SHAME GAME

The way to stop playing your partner's destructive game is to stop blaming and shaming yourself for being imperfect. You must also stop driving yourself to *do* better and *be* better—just to prove to him, yourself, and others that you are an acceptable, lovable, worthy human being.

You can feel strong and good about yourself whether your partner's accusations are true or untrue. And you can feel strong and good about yourself even if you are confused and unsure about the truth of his accusations. How? By learning to fully accept yourself and your intrinsic worth, no matter what. This may sound difficult, but you can do it by giving yourself one of REBT's most valuable gifts: unconditional self-acceptance. When you truly believe that you *are* okay no matter what is *said* about you or what is *true* about you, you will be able to

- Stop taking your partner's accusations to heart
- Stop feeling emotionally beaten up by your partner
- Stop beating yourself up
- Stop feeling "less than" and unlovable
- Stop desperately looking for proof that your partner is being hurtful and that you don't deserve it
- Let go of your overwhelming need to figure out what part, if any, of the negative things your partner says about you are true
- Give up your need to keep proving yourself to your partner, yourself, and others
- Stop feeling guilty for being who you are and doing what you do

You can learn to think and react like people who have a healthy level of self-acceptance and self-worth. They are able to make the distinction between "being" and "doing," so that what they do does not dictate their worth as a human being. They have granted themselves freedom from the realm of "less than." Here are some of the benefits they have derived:

- They are not devastated by negative comments made by others. They are able to consider the source, and when it is unreliable, they can discount the importance of what is said. They can ignore remarks when they are not true.
- They know they don't have to be perfect—that no one is. They recognize abuse as abuse and know that it is unwarranted, no matter what degree of truth there may be to some of their accuser's remarks.
- They can recognize when they are being treated abusively, and they are able to focus on dealing with it,

rather than diverting their attention to their flaws and mistakes and wasting precious energy beating themselves up.

• They are able to evaluate whether they might benefit from improving a behavior called to their attention by others, without feeling defensive; and they are able to take steps to change—not to satisfy someone else or to reduce the abuse—but to improve themselves, for themselves.

Okay, so it would be great to be able to believe that you are an acceptable, worthy, lovable person—no matter what. To be able to accept yourself, just as you are. To know that you have value that doesn't fluctuate with your successes and failures, or with anyone else's opinion of you. But how can achieve this? By changing your thinking. As we have pointed out before, it's not what your *partner* thinks, but what *you* think that counts. What *you* think that can make you very strong or very weak. What *you* think that makes the difference between being annoyed by your partner's criticisms and accusations or being devastated by them.

Actually, it's very simple. If you think bad thoughts about yourself, you will feel bad about yourself. If you think good thoughts about yourself, you will feel good about yourself. You have to be firm in your resolve to think in a manner that will serve your needs and heal your pain.

THE THINKING THAT WILL HELP YOU FEEL OKAY ABOUT YOURSELF NO MATTER WHAT!

How can you achieve a healthy level of self-acceptance and self-worth even though you are with a partner who is relentlessly grinding you down? How do you stop his inroads on your worth when you cannot stop his abuse? Obviously, by stopping *your own*. In plain English, you give up the *concept* of worthlessness and refuse to down yourself *no matter what*. Yes, you simply refuse to see yourself as less than okay or as a "bad" or worthless person, *under any conditions*. You give yourself *unconditional self-acceptance*. This will work whether your feelings of being "less than" seem to have originated with your partner or were deeply entrenched before he ever came on the scene.

Giving yourself unconditional self-acceptance is a major step toward reducing your emotional pain when you are in an abusive relationship. It creates a solid personality foundation that will help you be successful in many areas of your life and in your other relationships—with family members, friends, business or professional colleagues, service people. Here is how you can develop unconditional self-acceptance:

1. *You unconditionally accept yourself even when you are wrong.*

You recognize and acknowledge that, for the most part, your accuser is unjustly, nastily berating you, but you tell yourself, "In some ways he may be right. I may be doing some stupid, foolish things. I'm certainly fallible and imperfect! But even if I'm wrong, dead wrong, about this, even if I'm crazy about that, this and that are only my *behaviors*, they are not *me*. I am always an *acceptable, valid person* even when some of my *performances* are lacking. I *am* what I *am*—not what I *do*."

2. *You unconditionally accept yourself even when your partner verbally attacks you.*

You very much would like his approval and love. You would get great satisfaction and pleasure from it. But you don't *need it* to be happy; you have several other roads to enjoyment. And you especially don't *have to* make your *worth as a person* dependent on the approval and love of your abusive partner. You have worth in your own right. You are alive and kicking! Your worth is not contingent upon your accuser's endorsement—unless you foolishly and arbitrarily think that it is!

3. *You unconditionally accept yourself whether or not other people respect and honor you.*

You would *like* them to do so because their liking you has many pleasures and advantages. But, once again, you do not have to connect their acceptance to your own evaluation of yourself as a worthy person. If you do, you will go up and down on the seesaw of personal worth as one group accepts you and another does not; or as one group respects you today and fails to respect you tomorrow. When you grant others the power to think for you, you *disempower* yourself.

Accepting yourself unconditionally will solve many of your problems. But to be able to do this, you must get past the following things:

- Your inborn tendency to feel guilty and depressed when you think, or when you think others think, you have acted badly, wrongly, or stupidly
- Your habitual self-downing
- The cultural influences that train women to be subservient to men and make them less likely than men to stand up for their own rights, and more likely to apologize for their "mistakes"

Can you really get past all your old thinking and accept yourself unconditionally? Of course, because as you have learned, you have some remarkable abilities and talents on your side.

- You control your own feelings. You don't have to let them control *you*.
- You largely feel the way you think, and you can think about your thinking—and change it.
- "No one can insult you or put you down without your permission," as Eleanor Roosevelt said.
- Your verbal abuser has the power to physically harm you, but he cannot harm you mentally or emotionally unless you allow it.

GETTING RID OF SELF-BLAME AND GUILT THE REBT WAY

REBT is one of the few psychotherapies that takes a definite stand on self-blame and guilt: It is never legitimate or valid. What, *never*? Yes, *never*. To help you understand this unusual position, let us first define self-blame and guilt.

Think about the many things you do in your lifetime. Naturally you sometimes make mistakes and do things badly or wrong. You may, for example, say something in anger that you wish you hadn't. And some things you do may even be illegal or immoral. You may cheat on your taxes or not turn in a wallet or piece of jewelry you find. You have the choice of doing or not doing these socially bad acts. When you do them you are responsible for them, and responsible for the harm you may cause yourself and others. You can say that you are then acting irresponsibly and are guilty of your *acts*. You can legitimately feel this kind of guilt. It is appropriate to feel sorry, regretful, or remorseful about the harm you have done.

When abused people feel guilty, however, they do not merely acknowledge their responsibility for the things they do wrong and feel the healthy negative feelings of sorriness, regretfulness, and remorse. They blow their bad behavior out of proportion and take their guilt one step further. They think less of themselves as a *person* because of what they *did*. They believe, "I did badly and therefore I, as a person, am bad or worthless." This belief creates extreme unhealthy guilt and unhealthy self-defeating feelings of self-hatred, worthlessness, and self-damnation.

Being in a verbally abusive relationship provides numerous opportunities to do this. Just think of all the times you have felt extreme unhealthy guilt, hated yourself, and dwelled on your bad feelings. This, says REBT, you can certainly live without.

The solution to the problem of self-hatred is—again—for you to give yourself unconditional self-acceptance, no matter how badly you behave and how criticized you are for your behavior. If you didn't do something you are accused of, don't buy into it. If you *did* do it, accept responsibility, be appropriately sorry, but do not think that your *entire self* is no good because something you *did* wasn't good.

Why should you strive to achieve unconditional self-acceptance? Because it works!

CONDITIONAL SELF-ACCEPTANCE AND WHY IT DOESN'T WORK

If the only time you accept and like yourself is when you perform important things adequately and when you are approved of or loved by significant people, you are giving yourself *conditional* self-acceptance. It is a great feeling when you have it. But it is really quite problematic for several reasons:

1. *Conditional self-acceptance keeps your positive feelings about yourself on a perpetual roller coaster.*

Conditional self-acceptance means that you like yourself when you do well and tend to hate yourself when you do badly. It is based on such things as how well you do your job, how talented or smart you are, what you look like, and what other people think of you.

If you accept yourself only conditionally, where are you going to be when you make a mistake? Solidly into self-hatred. So your conditional self-acceptance—or self-esteem—goes up and down constantly. Now you have it; now you don't. And when you don't, you feel anxious, depressed, panicked, and other strong unhealthy feelings, because you are choosing to give yourself self-acceptance under only limited, and sometimes rare, conditions.

2. *Conditional self-acceptance will rarely help you do better, and will often cause you to do worse.*

Evaluating the various things you do and don't do is useful and life preserving. It helps you correct your mistakes and function better in the present and future. However, the self-downing you create when you demand that you *must* do well *to accept yourself*, and when you *berate* yourself when you don't do well, rarely helps you accomplish more or do better. In fact, the more you obsess over how good or how bad a *person* you are, the more anxious you will become. You will distract yourself from whatever you are doing and make it more difficult to do a good job. When you feel like a bad person and believe you can't do any better, you usually bring about the self-fulfilling prophecy of actually doing worse. When you focus on *what* you are doing rather than on how "good" or "bad" *you* are for doing it, you will tend to act more efficiently.

3. *Putting yourself down for doing poorly causes you to lose the respect of others—and invites poor treatment by them.*

Most people who see that you are putting *yourself* down, rather than your *behavior*, lose respect for you and see you in the same poor light in which you see yourself. How can they feel respect for someone who says "I'm so stupid! I always do that"? Some people—especially verbal abusers like your partner—enjoy your self-hatred, because, in comparison, they see themselves as "competent" and "good." When you are "one down," they are "one up." They also take advantage of your obvious vulnerability, make demands, and dish out hurtful treatment they wouldn't risk with people who have a higher opinion of themselves.

4. *More importantly, there is no way that you can give an accurate general or global rating to your self, your being, or your person.*

Think of the millions of things you do in your lifetime. How can you accurately judge each of them and come up with some kind of general evaluation of yourself as a "good" or a "bad" person? You can't. With your thoughts, feelings, and actions constantly changing, how can you possibly decide from one minute to the next whether you are "good" or "bad"? As long as you live, you are an ongoing process; and even if you could intelligently rate all your past and present acts, how do you know what you will do and how well you will do it in the future? You don't.

We could go on with the evils of rating yourself in global terms but as you can already see, it doesn't work. Our purpose is to help you stop doing it by giving you a workable solution: unconditional self-acceptance.

HOW TO DEVELOP *UNCONDITIONAL* SELF-ACCEPTANCE

REBT offers you a choice between two main philosophies of unconditional self-acceptance. You can decide which you would feel most comfortable adopting as your new way of viewing yourself. Both work—if you use them consistently.

Philosophy #1

"I refuse to give myself, my being, or my essence any kind of *global* or *general* rating. I will rate my thoughts, feelings, and behaviors only in terms of whether or not they help me achieve my basic goals and purposes."

If you adopt this philosophy, you never say, "I *am* good or I *am* bad." You stick to rating your thoughts, feelings, and behaviors in terms of whether or not they help you achieve your basic goals and purposes. But you refrain from rating your *self*, your personhood at all. You merely say: "I exist, and my goal is to continue to exist, and to be happy and relatively free from pain as I exist. So I will view it as good when I properly aid these goals, and I will view it as bad when I improperly sabotage them. But I will not give myself, my being, or my essence *any* general or global rating. It can't be done anyway and will only hurt me. I will unconditionally accept myself just because I am alive and human, and I will refrain from rating my total self or personhood as either good or bad."

Denise is an REBT client who recently adopted this view of herself. She wanted to lose fifteen pounds, so she decided to cut down her food portions and not eat sweets until she had lost the weight. One night, two weeks into her diet regimen, she went to her parent's house for dinner. For dessert they served chocolate cream pie—her favorite. She broke her pledge and ate a large piece.

Afterward, when she got home, she blamed herself for being weak. Then she remembered her new REBT philosophy. She said to herself, "Eating a piece of pie when I am trying to lose weight was not a good thing to do because it went against my goal of losing weight. But eating it didn't make me a bad person any more than not eating it other days made me a good person. It only made me a person who made a bad decision. All is not lost. I'll do better tomorrow."

Philosophy #2

"I will always define myself as a good or worthy individual— just because I exist, just because I am alive, just because I am human. I will not rate anything."

This is a simple but very practical solution. Thinking of yourself as good, worthy, or deserving of happiness "just because" has real advantages. It tends to make you feel joyful about living. It gives you a sense of self-confidence, supports your efforts to achieve important things, and helps you to perform much better. REBT teaches that you can achieve unconditional self-acceptance by merely believing: "I am a good person. I am worthy of living and enjoying, just because I am alive, just because I am human, just because I am me. I *choose* to see myself as a good person, so I *will*!"

When you adopt this philosophy, you can recognize that you have faults and make mistakes, but you can still insist, "I know that I am and will always be a good person. Why? Just because I exist! Just because I am alive and kicking!" You can thereby define yourself as good, even though you are verbally abused, even though you procrastinate, even though you foolishly smoke and eat too much—even though you aren't perfect.

Simple enough? Yes—and no. For an abused person, learning to assume you are acceptable just *as* you are, just *because* you are, is a foreign concept. But it works. All you have to do is choose to believe it and remind yourself of it again and again, until it becomes second nature to you. You can speed up this process by writing down your new philosophy and reviewing it often: "I am a good person. I am worthy of living and enjoying, just because I am alive, just because I am human, just because I am me. I *choose* to see myself as a good person, so I *will!*"

REBT's notion of unconditional self-acceptance, then, consists of either evaluating your behaviors in terms of how they succeed or fail to achieve your basic goals and purposes but not giving yourself or your being any kind of overall rating; or defining yourself as good and worthy just because you are alive and human, just because you choose to do so, and not rating anything. Take your choice—both of these philosophies of unconditional self-acceptance will work.

You may find it easier to simply accept yourself as good because you are alive and human. If instead you adopt the philosophy that includes rating your actions, be careful not to fall into the old habit of rating your *entire self*. Every time you are tempted to rate your entire being, strongly remind yourself that any kind of rating of your entire self is inaccurate and useless. And make up your mind that from now on, you will evaluate what you think, feel, and do—but not your entire self.

UNCONDITIONAL *OTHER* ACCEPTANCE CAN RELEASE YOU FROM THE ANGER THAT KEEPS YOU HOOKED INTO YOUR PARTNER AND YOUR PAIN

You have seen what happens when you damn yourself. Now let's consider what happens when you damn *other* people: You get angry! But you may not recognize it because anger can be experienced in different ways. Most people are familiar only with the obvious, outward kind. Anger, however, can be turned inward and experienced as depression, a more "acceptable" form of anger.

Or it may be experienced as pain and suffering. Regardless of the form it takes, your anger is hurting you. And it hurts you even more if you make yourself feel guilty and depressed about being angry. Anger keeps you emotionally hooked into your partner and his erratic behavior. It sabotages your efforts to cope and can make you very sick.

If you continue to damn others and put them down, you can easily build your anger into a roaring rage and hatred that harms you much more than those who are the objects of your fury. Or you can slip into a depression so severe that everything seems hopeless and you even consider taking your own life. As you can see, like damning yourself, damning other people creates destructive emotions. The REBT answer is to give up your absolutistic musts, shoulds, oughts, and demands, and give people the other side of the unconditional self-acceptance coin: unconditional *other* acceptance. And, as uncomfortable as it may be to hear, that includes your verbally abusive partner.

If this makes you cringe and want to shout "No way!" remember that REBT is showing you the best way to achieve your goals of reducing your emotional pain, becoming better able to deal with your abusive partner, and feeling calm, centered, and strong enough to make rational decisions.

Just as you have learned to separate *your* behavior from *your* entire being, you have to learn to separate your *partner's* behavior from *his* entire being. You need to fully accept and completely give up damning *anyone*—in spite of abusive or other obnoxious behavior. Believe it or not, you can refrain from judging others, including your partner, the same way you have learned to refrain from judging yourself.

Why should you even consider not judging and damning your partner when his behavior is so deplorable? Because, once again, judging and damning him results in your developing anger—anger that, no matter how justified it may seem, only tears you up and does nothing to reduce the abuse or punish your partner. You may have to deal with *his* anger 75 percent of the time, but you have to deal with *your* anger 100 percent of the time.

When we suggest you not view your abusive partner as *all* bad and *totally* damnable, we are not suggesting that you excuse his atrocious behavior. And we are certainly not suggesting that you focus on his redeeming characteristics or acts instead, which you probably already do—to a fault. We are simply following the REBT model of not damning yourself or anyone else because it causes anger and hate that works against your own goal of not becoming extremely upset. You feed your rage every time you tell yourself how damnable your partner is and that he *should not* be that way. Learning to stop damning your partner in his totality, his entire self, his essence, and giving him unconditional other acceptance are completely and totally for *your* benefit—not *his*. It is not anything you have to tell him. It is a private process that goes on in your own mind, for your own good.

Remember, in abusive situations, the person who remains calm and rational usually "wins." And remaining calm and rational is the choice you make when you decide to stop your damning and hating. When you rile yourself up over your partner's abusive behavior, you give him the power to keep you hooked into his psychological storms. Only when you are coolheaded and rational will you be able to confront him in a way that stands a chance of being effective.

Your ultimate victory is in taking back the power to dictate your own emotions and to use your free will to make choices that enhance your life and bring you inner peace.

Once you decide to give yourself the gifts of unconditional self-acceptance and unconditional other-acceptance, you will have begun to take back your power. And you will have taken a major step toward gaining control of your emotions and your life.

In the next chapter, we will use examples of common problems experienced by abused partners to show you how to use your new non-judgmental, give-yourself-a-break philosophy in your daily life—even when the going gets rough.

Your Practical New Philosophy In Action

Now let's see how the REBT techniques and philosophies you have learned can help you solve problems in your daily life. We use examples of common problems to "think" you through and "talk" you through these techniques. And we teach you an effective method you can use to make difficult decisions about staying or leaving your relationship, or about almost anything else.

Although your problems may be somewhat different from those we talk about, the rational way of looking at them—including the use of unconditional self-acceptance, disputing, and healthy self-talk—can be applied to almost any problem you have.

You will get ideas for healthy self-talk you can use quickly in "emergency" situations. Then you will learn how to do shortcut disputing, a technique that will help you build an emotional fortress to protect you whenever you need it, wherever you are.

COMMON PROBLEMS AND THEIR REBT ANSWERS

Problem: *You feel fat, ugly, boring, or stupid, and are afraid that if your partner leaves you, or you leave him, no one else would ever want you.*

Answer: Just because you *feel* fat, ugly, boring, or stupid, doesn't mean that you *are*. You may feel this way because you have been beaten down by your abusive partner, or you may have felt this way ever since you can remember. What can you do? Begin by disputing your irrational belief that *feeling* fat, ugly, boring, or stupid *proves* that you *are*. Show yourself that just because you feel this way doesn't make it true.

But what if there is some truth to how you feel? Maybe you have felt so bad about yourself for so long that you find it difficult to make conversation with people. Or maybe you *are* overweight. Then what? You can remind yourself of your new unconditional self-acceptance philosophy. You are not your appearance, your personality, your knowledge. You are not what you say or do, or don't say or do. You are not what other people think of you. You can accept yourself as you are while recognizing that there may be some things about you that you would like to improve.

You have been so busy focusing on your bad points that you probably have not thought about your good qualities for a long time. There is no law that says you have to do that. In fact, it might be an interesting experience to focus on your *good* qualities for a change and see what happens. You might be able to accept a compliment with a smile and a thank you. (You can learn to feel better about yourself by reading my [M.G.P.'s] book *Charisma: How to get "that special magic."*)

What you think of yourself shows in your attitude, in your facial expression, in the way you carry yourself. A positive body language makes a stronger statement than some extra pounds or crooked teeth. So if you think that no one will ever want or love you because your ears stick out or your complexion isn't perfect, or because you aren't the best informed or most highly educated or stimulating person on the face of the earth, look around. Not everyone is thin, beautiful, fascinating, and brilliant. In fact, most people are ordinary, yet millions of them find someone to love who loves them in return. And so do many physically challenged people who face obstacles just getting through each day.

All kinds of people with all kinds of traits manage to establish happy, satisfying relationships and find partners who appreciate their essential goodness, their sense of humor, their adventurous nature, their values, their worldview, and their idiosyncrasies. You, too, can find someone to love you—just because you are you.

Problem: *What can you do when you get that shaky feeling and you know that there is some truth to what your partner is yelling at you about? And how do you stop blaming yourself?*

Answer: As we have said, most of the things your partner attacks you for are completely irrational and have no basis in fact. Generally, it is best not to even listen to the poison daggers that fly out of his mouth. But as every abused partner knows, these twisted untruths are sometimes interspersed with truths and partial truths.

If you remember your decision to give yourself unconditional self-acceptance and view your flaws and mistakes as part of being human, you will be able to stop upsetting yourself. You will recognize that *everyone* has faults and makes mistakes, yet no one deserves to be abused for them.

So stop putting yourself down, stop believing that your shortcomings cause your partner's abusive behavior, and get out of the habit of focusing—or obsessing—on his criticism. You indeed may have some shortcomings. And they may be harmful to you, your partner, your children, and others. But even though old habits are hard to break, you can almost always learn how to reduce or remove them.

Begin by being completely honest with yourself. Recognize that you may not be doing the best you can in certain areas. Don't deny your flaws, insist they are minor, or rationalize them away. Doing so will only set you up to feel guilty and will do nothing to help you respect yourself or grow into a happier person. To the extent that your partner is rightly criticizing what you do, but wrongly damning you for doing it, you can use his criticism constructively to work on yourself.

Once you are crystal clear about what is really going on and you are feeling better and coping better, you have the option of unemotionally evaluating whether you might benefit from improving a behavior called to your attention by your abuser—not to satisfy him or to reduce the abuse or to justify it—but to improve yourself, for yourself.

If you decide to work on one of your flaws, fully acknowledge it to yourself without grossly exaggerating it. Examine the thoughts, feelings, and actions that accompany it.

Tell yourself, for example, "Yes, it's true that I don't keep the house very neat. I pick up here and there mainly when the mess gets so bad that I begin having difficulty finding things or when someone is coming over. Let me see what I am doing to create this mess. Hmm…I don't hang up my clothes when I take them off and I don't often put things away after I use them. I tell myself, 'I'll clean it all up tomorrow.' I'm a pack rat, too. I'm not very good at throwing out old magazines, newspapers, or mail. I even have trouble getting rid of old clothes that I don't wear anymore. Hmm!"

As you note the details of some of your own shortcomings, look for the irrational beliefs that encourage you to create them. In the case of being untidy about your house, for example, your irrational beliefs might well be: "I'm too tired and upset to straighten up. It's *too hard* to keep cleaning up things, especially when everything will get all messed up again, anyway. What a pain! I hate picking stuff up. Besides, I'm so busy with other things that I don't have the time."

Look at these irrational beliefs, dispute them actively and vigorously, and change them into an effective new philosophy. Assuming there are no extenuating circumstances that take priority over keeping your home neat, you can acknowledge your shortcomings and say something to yourself like, "Although my partner is wrong in condemning me and there is no excuse for the cruel way in which he does it, he happens to be right this time about my keeping the house messy. I would actually like to keep it neater. So, no excuses! I know that with a little effort I do a much better job than I have been. But I am not a slob, as he so wrongly accuses me. I am a person who is not keeping my home as neat as I might. I see that my behavior is not good and could be improved. So, without blaming my entire being for my flaws, I am going to do my best to correct them. Let's see how well I can do this. And even if I don't somehow do so, I still won't view myself as an incompetent person. My bad behavior doesn't equal a bad me." Disputing this way will help you change behavior you don't like in yourself. Then you will be able to correct some of your shortcomings much easier.

Of course there may be extenuating circumstances. You may, for example, have been ill, or working and going to school, and have little time to clean up the house. If you also have small children, you have even less time. In such cases you could recognize that you had to establish priorities and forgive yourself for not keeping things as neat as you would like.

Using REBT, you learn to see yourself as a person with definite flaws rather than as a thoroughly flawed, and therefore unworthy, person. When the situation warrants it, you give yourself permission to temporarily continue what might be considered less than desirable behavior under usual conditions. The point is that when there is something you can change, do it. When there is something you can't change, do the best you can. The important thing is to be honest with yourself without blaming or damning your entire self.

Problem: *You have thought about the advantages and disadvantages of confronting your partner about his abuse. You have decided that there are goc . reasons for doing so, but you are afraid because you think you would be unable to stand his reaction. You consider this a weakness on your part. You keep putting yourself down and mercilessly beating yourself up because of your fear. How do you stop criticizing yourself and making yourself feel guilty and worthless for being afraid?*

Answer: Criticizing yourself and making yourself feel guilty and worthless for being afraid of confronting your partner is no different from criticizing yourself and feeling guilty and worthless for any other behavior. It only makes your situation worse.

Put the energy you are using—and wasting—on beating yourself up into accepting yourself and your human frailties. Remember what REBT has taught you: You *are* not what you *do*—or *don't* do. Self-blame and guilt are never legitimate.

Use your new unconditional self-acceptance philosophy: "Being afraid to confront my partner doesn't make me a weak or worthless person. It only makes me a person who is acting weakly right now. By berating myself for this weakness, I will only make myself weaker and cause myself even more pain. My self-damnation is self-defeating! It keeps me too weak to take action. Let me keep looking at my weakness, considering how to change it, and reminding myself that things won't change unless I start doing something to help change them. But, if I can't bring myself to do anything right now, I still won't put myself down. I refuse to beat myself up over it."

Problem: *You have been confronting your partner about his verbal abuse. He has not stopped it; perhaps it has increased and grown more severe. You now are seriously contemplating leaving him but are indecisive because there are still good reasons for your staying with him, at least for now. What can you do to help yourself make a decision?*

Answer: There is a practical method that can help you come to a decision about leaving. It is called hedonic calculus, modeled after the suggestions of an early 19th century philosopher, Jeremy Bentham. It is a list of advantages and disadvantages rated according to their importance. It will help you evaluate your situation from a rational point of view, rather than an emotional one.

Take a few days to make a list of the practical advantages and the practical disadvantages of staying with your partner in spite of his continued verbal abuse. This will require you to separate your practical reasons for staying from your emotional ones. (Your emotional reasons will be dealt with in the following two chapters.)

Advantages of staying, for example, might include the following:

- Having some companionship from my partner
- Keeping the family intact for the children
- Saving the expense of living apart
- Avoiding the disruption in my life that would be caused by leaving
- Giving me time to obtain job training or go back to school

Disadvantages of staying might include the following:

- Not having the continuous, loving companionship I want
- Living with criticism and blame
- Feeling ill as a result of the continuous stress
- Being turned off to him sexually (or not having any sex)
- The children suffering from living with abuse

Carefully consider every advantage and disadvantage on your list, and give each a rating from one to ten. For example, using our list, you may rate "the children suffering from living with abuse" as a ten, "saving the expense of living apart" as a seven, and "having some companionship from my partner" as a three. When you have rated all the advantages and disadvantages on your own list in terms of the pleasure and pain you would feel if they were to occur, add up your ratings on both sides to see which side comes out higher. Repeat the rating process on several different days to see how consistent your results are. You may also want to review your list to make sure you haven't forgotten anything important.

If you consistently get a similar numerical result, it will help you see your situation more clearly. If you get a total of 105 for the advantages of staying with your partner, for instance, and a total of 76 for the disadvantages of staying, you will know that you would probably be better off staying. Suppose, however, that your list indicates you and your family would be much better off leaving your partner, but you still don't have enough strength to carry out this decision. What can you do? You can first review your reasons for staying and try to change the reasoning behind them. If, for example, you are convincing yourself to stay mainly because you want to keep the family intact for the children, you can reexamine this and show yourself that

- Keeping the family intact means keeping the children in an abusive environment
- Living in an abusive environment causes the children to be anxious, fearful, and angry
- Neither an abusive father nor a submissive mother is a good role model for children
- If the children don't live in a loving household, it will be difficult for them to create one of their own as an adult

If disputing the advantages of staying doesn't make you stronger in your resolve to leave, you can recognize that your weak behavior isn't good, without denigrating your self, your personhood, or your being. You can constantly tell yourself, "My procrastination and my inertia about leaving my partner is harmful, bad, and foolish, but it never makes me a bad person. I am just a fallible human who is now displaying some of my fallibility. If I condemn myself for this, I will just make myself more anxious and weaker. I am determined to fully accept myself with my failings. Then I will be able to more calmly observe exactly what they are and change my thinking and actions so as to improve them. But even if I never correct my indecision and weakness, and if I stay with my abusive partner forever, I am still a person who behaves poorly but *never*, *never* a bad person."

HEALTHY SELF-TALK FOR "EMERGENCY" SITUATIONS

In stressful situations, you resort to what you know best. And, unfortunately, what you know best is *unhealthy* self-talk. You have probably used it every day of your life for years. You have lived with the mental traffic jams it causes when you most need to think clearly. *Healthy* self-talk, on the other hand, helps you cope effectively. With practice, you can make healthy self-talk your new automatic way of thinking, even when you are under stress.

Here are some common situations that trigger unhealthy self-talk in abused partners. Let's see what healthy self-talk you can use instead.

Problem: *Your partner is a Dr. Jekyll and Mr. Hyde. He changes from being calm and nice to being irritable, or angry and mean, without warning. You can seldom enjoy whatever good times there are because you are anxiously anticipating what will happen next. What can you say to yourself in this situation?*

New Self-talk: "I refuse to spend every minute of my life worrying about his moods. I would prefer that he not become angry and give me a hard time, but that's what he does. I now know it's not the end of the world, especially if I don't contribute to it by thinking about it all the time. I *choose*—even if I have to force myself at first—to think about other things rather than scaring myself about the outburst to come."

Problem: *Your partner has erupted again and angrily walked out or gone to sleep. You are left with his words ringing in your ears. What can you say to yourself to deal with your feelings?*

New Self-talk: "There he goes again, doing 'his thing'— throwing a tantrum and running away. He's not even here to hurt me anymore. I'm keeping myself in pain. This is going to stop here and now. I will not let him ruin my day nor will I ruin my own day. And I refuse to have one more sleepless night. Whatever he thinks, he thinks. Whatever he does, he does. It's not my problem and I'm not *making* it my problem. I *choose* to stop thinking about it right this minute. I will read, take a bath, or take the children to the park, and I will think only about things that make me feel good."

Problem: *Your partner seems to somehow ruin every joyous occasion. Every time you are happy and feeling good, he somehow finds a way to bring you down. What can you possibly say to yourself in this situation?*

New Self-talk: "That's enough! I absolutely refuse to allow him to ruin this moment. It's happened too many times already. I won't let his behavior control how I feel. I am happy. I feel good. And I'm going to stay this way! I won't let anything he says or does spoil this for me! I *choose* to remain untouched by his behavior. I will concentrate on my good feelings and push thoughts of him out of my mind."

Problem: *"You have tried to stop thinking about what your partner said, but you can't. Trying to think about other things has not worked. Trying to keep busy hasn't worked either. You are angry with yourself because you can't stop obsessing. What can you say to yourself in this situation?*

New Self-talk: "I will not beat myself up for obsessing. This is the way my mind is accustomed to helping me work out my problems. But now I know that obsessing will only keep me too upset to think clearly. I am learning a new rational way to think that will help me find real solutions. In the meantime, instead of continuing to obsess and upset myself, I will immediately write down my irrational thoughts and dispute them. When my emotions are no longer running wild, the things I'm obsessing about will seem less important. This will stop the thoughts from racing around in my mind."

Can you see how much better you will feel when you get used to talking to yourself in a healthy way? In time it will become easier, and your feelings of being back in control will grow stronger.

It may be difficult at first to think up healthy self-talk when you need it most. Therefore, when things are calm, write it down and keep copies in easily accessible places, such as your nightstand and purse. (If you feel you must keep these reminders hidden, make sure you know where they are and can get to them when you need them.) Reread your healthy self-talk until you truly believe it. During the bad times, when you can't remember what to say, use your written self-talk to help you cope with your feelings. Eventually, being able to think of appropriate healthy self-talk will become automatic.

SHORTCUT DISPUTING

Once you have had some practice disputing and know what healthy self-talk sounds like, you can often use a shortcut method to change your old irrational thoughts to new rational ones—without having to go through all the usual disputing steps. How can you do this? By taking the kinds of things you have been telling yourself when you dispute your irrational beliefs and using them as shortcut versions of your effective new philosophies.

Let's say your partner blames you for something—not an unusual occurrence. You dispute it and come up with an effective new philosophy. Some of the statements in your philosophy can be used to remind you of the entire disputing process. In REBT we call these short statements rational coping self-statements.

If you dispute weakly, your effective new philosophies will be weak and so will your coping statements. Weak statements will not produce lasting results. Here's what a weak one sounds like: "It's not my fault I'm being abused, even though my partner says it is. It really isn't. And I'm not a terrible person."

If you dispute strongly your effective new philosophies will be strong and so will your coping statements. Strong statements will produce lasting results. Here is what a strong one sounds like: "I *absolutely*, *positively* am *not* responsible for the abuse, no matter *what* my partner says! It's *not* my fault! And I am *not* a terrible person! I'm *not*, I'm *not*, I'm *not*!"

See the difference? You need to make your coping statements vigorous, forceful, and empowering to get the results you want.

Write down your coping statements and reread them

frequently, just as you are going to do with your healthy self-talk. When you have the privacy, read them aloud, forcefully repeating them many times. Do this as often as you can—at least three times a day—even when things are going well for the time being. Be relentless with yourself. Think them through again and again and recall them frequently throughout the day, using them as you would affirmations. Go over them until you fully believe them. Repetition will help you memorize your coping statements, so you have them at your fingertips.

Then, as soon as you begin to feel upset, quickly substitute one of your coping statements for the irrational things you are saying to yourself. Usually, your unhealthy feelings will rapidly shift to healthy ones. The more you drum your coping statements into your head and heart, the sooner you will fully embrace the REBT philosophy, and the faster—and better—it will work for you in times of need. After a little practice, the right statement will pop into your mind and replace the unhealthy nonsense you are telling yourself. It's so easy, and so empowering!

Rational coping statements help you refocus your thoughts, quickly remind you of your new philosophy, and reinforce your new habit of thinking rationally. They will become an important part of your new self-talk; self-talk from a new, supportive inner best friend, instead of from the old, self-sabotaging inner enemy you have been listening to for far too long. You will be amazed at how much better you will feel and how much easier it will be to behave in a healthier, more rational way.

Here are some examples of coping statements to get you started:

- "My partner is usually going to act the way *he* wants—not the way *I* want. Too bad!"
- "I do not *need* what I *want*—especially my partner's verbal approval—though I strongly *prefer* it."
- "He cannot insult or upset me without my *letting* him."
- "*He* can't make me hurt. Only *I* can."
- "Even if I may be *acting* weakly by not standing up to him or by staying with him, I *am* never a weak, inadequate *person*."

- "Being abused is a real problem and I may have many difficulties because of it, but I positively *refuse* to make them into holy horrors!"
- "It isn't awful. It's just *too bad*. Too bad I can deal with."
- "I absolutely *refuse* to upset myself about this for one more second! Being upset only makes things worse."
- "I positively *will not* allow myself to analyze what happened. It doesn't matter. Abuse is abuse!"
- "Stop it! I *will not* put myself down! I *am* not what I *do*! I am a good, worthy person—no matter what!"

Once you become comfortable using rational coping self-statements to support your effective new philosophies, you can abbreviate your statements even further. Think up some easy-to-memorize one-line sayings to use that express the same ideas as your coping statements. Rhymes and jungles are particularly helpful because they stick in your mind. Use these one-liners quietly as mantras, or shout them so you hear the messages loud and clear. Get into the habit of repeating them to yourself throughout the day.

You can also call upon these little gems to carry you through difficult times, such as when your partner creates one of his usual "scenes," when you begin to obsess, or when you just feel bad. They can short-circuit your pain-producing thinking and instantly get you back into a rational mode. Learn those we suggest or make up some of your own. Then repeat them to yourself again and again with conviction whenever you feel the need.

- "Oh well, there he goes again, doing his 'thing.'"
- "I refuse to waste one more minute of my life hurting over this!"
- "I am powerful when I *think* I am."
- "He can *blame* me but he can't *shame* me!"
- "He's *mad*. I'm *sad*. But I'm not *bad*!"
- "He acts like a *nut*.
  But I don't have to feel it in my *gut*."
- "I'm okay. He's *not* okay."
- "I'm not *buying* what he's *selling*!"
- "He's *mean*. I'm *leaving* this scene!"

- "I give myself the *blessing* of not *obsessing*."
- "I am the boss of me,
  I say how I will be."
- "I think I might, I think I may
  Make this Be-Kind-to-Myself Day."
- "My sweet little self I will mend
  By being my own very best friend."

I (M.G.P.) can't tell you how many times I have called upon these instant rational coping self-statements to help me through the ups and downs of my life. Yet, it still amazes me that uttering one little phrase or one little sentence can so rapidly and so completely change the way I feel about whatever is going on. Words hold such power. Coping statements have helped me to let go, accept what is, put things in perspective, and so much more.

One coping statement I use frequently has had a big impact on my life. It has repeatedly kept me from unnecessarily upsetting myself with the words *awful* and *terrible*. When I first learned how destructive these words can be and began listening to my self-talk and everyday speech, I was amazed at how often I was using them.

For years now, when I forget and begin telling myself that something is awful or terrible, I catch myself immediately and playfully say, "Well…it's not really *a-w-f-u-l*. It's just too bad." Then I smile inside, reminded that I have the power to decide how I will feel. Even when something *very, very* bad happens, I can cope with it better by not telling myself that it is awful and terrible, and that I can't stand it. Using coping statements has helped me deal with difficult situations and events in my life, both big and small.

You, too, can use these REBT shortcuts to take control of your emotions. They are wonderful tools you can use for the rest of your life. Imagine how much less upset you would be when your partner acts out, if you could say calmly and with conviction: "There he goes again. He's off and running—but not with me!" Then you, too, could smile inside knowing that you have the power to decide how you will feel.

YOUR NEW PHILOSOPHY OF LIFE

If you keep disputing and using your shortcuts and healthy self-talk, you will feel better about yourself and be considerably less vulnerable to your verbally abusing partner—and, of course, to other abusers. But that's not all. You will also begin to create a general, overall new way of looking at every aspect of your life.

This general new philosophy develops quite naturally as you do your disputing and show yourself again and again what kind of thinking works—and what kind doesn't. Being able to manage your emotions and live a life based on reason becomes part of you and carries you through even the most stressful events.

Even if you have chosen to stay in your abusive relationship, your disputing will guide you to this new philosophy. And before you know it, you will believe what you have been saying to yourself:

"I strongly dislike my partner's abuse and I am determined to use whatever *healthy* means I can to try to stop it. I will also limit my exposure to it—and my children's—by staying away from it whenever possible. I will continue to reduce my unhealthy negative emotions about my abuse by practicing the ABCs of Emotions. Right now, however, for my own reasons, I'll stay and put up with his abuse—as long as it's not physical. He's wrong in being abusive. So he's wrong! Just because he's wrong doesn't mean I have to be miserable. If I don't take his abuse too seriously, I may be able to enjoy some aspects of him and our relationship in spite of his unfairness. If I can, fine. If I can't, that's okay too. Either way, I can definitely lead a happy life—though I would be much happier if he stopped being abusive.

"Any time his behavior begins to get to me, I will remind myself that I have chosen not to create pain over this. I will not let his anger prevent me from feeling good or living my life. I will love myself, be tender with myself, and fill my days with people who care and share. I will celebrate my uniqueness and my inner power. I will open a window in my mind so I can see that there are birds out there singing, stars twinkling, and flowers that bloom each spring."

If you have decided to leave, you will be saying something like this to yourself instead:

"I have tried everything I can think of to make my situation better and nothing has worked. I have also done everything I can to make myself feel better, and I do. But it is not enough. I don't want every day to be an effort. I have the rest of my life to live and I won't settle for crumbs. I want to try for the whole cake. I want love that doesn't hurt. I want tenderness that doesn't bite. I want caring and sharing—and I want peace.

"Even though leaving and starting a new life is difficult, I will remind myself that I am willing to go through temporary discomfort. At least that kind of discomfort will come to an end. I will find love again. In the meantime, I will love myself, be tender with myself, and fill my days with people who care and share. I will create a life that celebrates my uniqueness, my inner power, and my ability to choose how I will live. I will joyfully open my heart to the birds that sing, the stars that twinkle, and the flowers that bloom each spring."

You have seen how to put REBT philosophy and techniques into action. And you have learned how unconditionally accepting yourself and talking to yourself in a healthy way can change your world. In the next two chapters you will discover ways to overcome the fears that can paralyze your efforts to make rational decisions about your relationship, your life, and your future.

PART IV

Getting Past the Fears and Anxieties That Keep You Stuck

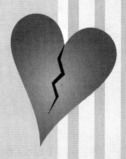

No More Staying for the Wrong Reasons or Suffering After You Have Left

Chapter 12

Overcoming the Three Biggest
Fears of Leaving

Fear can keep you in a relationship that you could and would otherwise leave. It is important that you be able to evaluate your situation without fears clouding your vision. It is the only way you will be able to see clearly and logically what you want your relationship and your life to be. And it is the only way you will be able to make a rational—rather than an emotional—decision about whether you are willing to do what it takes to change them.

Sometimes there are valid reasons for staying. Only you can decide. But whether you ultimately decide to stay or leave, you still have to overcome your fears. For as long as you have fears about leaving, they—rather than reason—will dictate your decision. If you overcome your fears and still choose to stay, you will be doing it because you rationally believe that it is in your best interest. If you overcome your fears and decide to leave, being free of them will make possible the peace of mind you are leaving your relationship to find. It will make building your new life an exciting adventure, rather than an anxiety-riddled chore.

This chapter discusses three of the fears abused partners find most disturbing and guides you through the "thinking" and "doing" steps it takes to get rid of them. Let's begin with the one that looms larger than life for most women: the fear of being alone.

THE FEAR OF BEING ALONE

You would think that verbally abused women would, at least temporarily, be glad to be alone—to be free of their partner's attacks. But millions are so afraid of being by themselves and of the possibility of facing painful years of aloneness that they frequently stay with the worst possible kinds of partners.

What they don't realize is that, in every way that counts, they are *already* alone. Perhaps the worst kind of alone is being *with* someone who isn't there—isn't there to consistently love you, appreciate you, understand you, and be a friend to you. You have undoubtedly felt this kind of aloneness. Your unloving partner may be so close you could reach out and touch him, yet so far that he seems miles away.

Obviously, keeping your partner in your life doesn't guarantee you steady love or companionship. It only guarantees you more abuse. Would it really be so much worse if you were by yourself? Think about it. No more put-downs, no more tumult, no more settling for "crumbs" of love, no more wishing and waiting your life away. And, you would be free to look for another partner who is capable of giving and receiving *real* love. Love that enhances your life. Love that is a reliable source of joy instead of misery. Love that is full and satisfying rather than empty and frustrating.

Leslie is a REBT client who was finally able to face her fear of being alone. She had felt so empty and worthless without a full-time man that from the age of 18 until she married at 30, she was rarely without a partner for more than a few weeks at a time. When Leslie was in a relationship she felt complete, and life was worthwhile. When she was not in a relationship, she felt empty, worthless, and utterly alone. So, although Leslie had a good job and could afford to be independent, her horror of being alone was so acute that she repeatedly gravitated toward and settled for some very unsuitable partners.

Tom seemed different. She met him when he came to her rescue after she was in an auto accident. He was one of the paramedics who took her to the emergency hospital. Their attraction was immediate and intense. When she was released with only minor injuries, he was waiting for her. Soon she was swept up in a whirlwind of romance. He wined her and dined her and bought her thoughtful little gifts. He was wonderful; he was charming; and he was persistent. He called her frequently and wanted to see her almost every day. Then they began living together. After two months he wanted to marry her. Her friends told her that it was too much, too soon, and she knew they were probably right, but she was "in love" and afraid that if she didn't do what he wanted, he would leave her and she would be alone again. And that she couldn't face.

After they were married, Tom sometimes acted like a different person—an irritable stranger. At those times he would criticize Leslie for everything—talking too much or talking too little, doing too much or doing too little. The more pressure he had at work, the more verbally abusive he became.

The good times became less and less frequent, yet she hung on to them for dear life. If she hadn't, she might have had reason to consider leaving. Even though she had a good job of her own, no children, and could take care of herself financially, every time the thought of living alone entered her head she panicked.

If she had merely had a strong desire to be in a love relationship, Leslie would have been all right. She could have left Tom and enjoyed dating different men until she met "Mr. Right." But she didn't *desire*—she *needed*—a love relationship on a day-to-day basis. Without it she was alone, terribly alone. And empty, terribly empty.

So Leslie stayed with Tom and suffered through his verbal abuse. The solution? To change her *dire need* to be in a relationship into merely a *strong desire*. Her two strong—very strong—*musts* were "I *must* always have a steady partner, or that proves that I am an inadequate, worthless person" and "I feel so empty and utterly alone without a man that I *must* have one, I *need* one, and I cannot *stand it* when I don't have one. I can't bear the thought of not having a man; it would be just too *awful*."

Let's see how REBT therapy helped Leslie see her needs differently, make new and better choices, and turn her life around.

I (A.E.) tackled Leslie's two *musts* by first showing her that although establishing a healthy relationship with a man is a worthy goal, her worth as a human being does not depend on it. I told her that she needs the love, attention, and approval of someone else to make her feel worthwhile because she doesn't *feel* worthwhile herself. When she feels better about herself and fully accepts herself as she is, she will not feel so utterly alone and empty without a man. She may *want* and *enjoy* being with a man—but not *need* to be.

I explained to her the two philosophies of unconditional self-acceptance. She could choose to view herself as a good person just because she *is*, or she could choose to view herself as neither a good nor bad person—whether or not she succeeds at attaining her goal of being in a relationship with a man.

As for the discomfort of being alone and not having a man, I told her: "It is a perfectly legitimate feeling since you like being part of a couple. But if you don't have what you wish to have, it isn't *awful* and you can *stand* it. There are many other pleasures in life. So you don't *have to* get what you want and don't *have to* make yourself utterly miserable when you fail to get it. You can be sorry about not being with a man right now, but having a steady companion is just desirable—not necessary! When you are no longer desperate for a partner, friendships will keep you from feeling alone. And when you find a new love, it will be because you *want* him, not because you *need* him."

When Leslie and I disputed her old irrational belief that she *must* have a man to be worthwhile and disputed her dire need to have one, she was able to leave Tom. Having a man like him was hardly an accomplishment; it was a detriment. And it certainly didn't make her a worthwhile human.

She decided to accept herself as a valid person regardless of how much she ever did or did not accomplish. As she adopted that philosophy, she started to achieve more than she ever had before. She developed new interests, made interesting friends, and soon had her pick of several suitable men. Meanwhile, since for the time being she had no steady partner, she was sorry and disappointed when she came home to an empty apartment, but she was hardly devastated—and she didn't feel empty. She still *wanted* a man in her life but no longer *needed* one.

You Can Want a Man in Your Life Without Needing One

If you are still with an abusive man because of your great fear of being alone, you can—instead of believing that you absolutely *need* a partner—repeatedly remind yourself of these things until you are strongly convinced:

1. *Your worth as a person depends on you, not on the love of other people, and certainly not on their cruel companionship.*

You have worth just because you are you, whether or not you have a partner. When you accept yourself unconditionally, you will not need the approval of others in order to feel worthwhile.

2. *If you leave, you will miss the fairy tale more than the reality.*

Staying with your abusive partner is hanging on to a fairy tale that isn't coming true. It is living an illusion. If you were to leave, would you really miss spending most of your time feeling bad and settling for crumbs? Is that what you want forever after? Believe it or not, you have a better chance of filling your emptiness by being alone than by being with your abusive partner.

3. *Your partner is not the "only one" for you.*

You may believe that if you leave, you would be losing the one true love of your life. That you would never again have the excitement and passion you think you need. That your partner has some magical quality that makes you forever connected to him. Often, however, a passion this intense is actually an addiction that is mistaken for love.

If you think your partner is the *only* person in the world you can love or enjoy sexually, you are hooked on an assumption, not a fact, and you will make it true until you give it up. It is just part of an imaginary love story you have created.

Another REBT client, Ellen, used disputing techniques to change her unhealthy thinking. She believed that Peter was the only man for her. It was the basis of her addiction to him. Even though she was being verbally abused, she was paralyzed by the thought of not having him in her life.

In therapy, Ellen learned what to do. She began by vigorously telling herself, scores of times: "I do *not* need Peter in my life. I do not *need* what I want. I like it, I *prefer* it, but it is only my insistence on needing it that makes it indispensable to me."

Gradually she turned her addiction to Peter into a strong desire to be with him. *Wanting* to be with him rather than *needing* to be made her stronger and less dependant. She was able to cope better with her relationship knowing that staying was a choice and that Peter was not the only man she could ever love.

4. You can get along fine by yourself.

Certainly there are advantages to having a man around. But you can also be comfortable by yourself, although in a different way. You can do almost everything you want to do—see friends, pursue interests, travel. You can go to work, manage your finances, raise your kids—all without the help of a partner.

Although it would probably be easier with help, you don't absolutely *need* it. You won't die without it. You can bear aloneness and still manage your life and enjoy yourself most of the time. In fact, you will have more freedom and most likely more fun without someone polluting your life with anxiety and pain.

5. Just because you are alone doesn't mean that you have to remain loveless, companionless, or without sex.

Being alone is not easy or without pain at the beginning, but your life is not easy or painless now. The important thing is that when you are alone, there is an end to the pain. It is amazing how relieved you can feel when there is no one to upset you and tear you apart, how quickly you can learn to enjoy the peace and quiet, and how soon you will find new adventures and new people to fill the old void.

You may think that you can't enjoy yourself unless you are with a man—that the things you do don't count somehow. A sunset is not as beautiful; a heart-to-heart talk is not as satisfying; and a vacation is not a "real" vacation without a man. But being alone doesn't mean that you can't have someone to share daily events with, that the beauty of the world is lessened, or that you must do without lighthearted fun, good companionship, and romance forever. It means that you have to, for now, change your focus from romantic love to other fulfilling types of love.

We can tell you—as your friends may have—that you do not have to remain alone. There are billions of people in the world, about half of them adults. Many want companionship and love as much as you do. Some are interested in the same things you are: books, movies, music, exercise. You can make new friends by getting out and looking for them. Attend classes and join groups, clubs, and organizations. Attend events for single people. Companionship is there—not merely for the *asking*, but for the *persisting*. And persisting will help you find your special someone.

Even your fear of being without sex for a while will not be catastrophic because the "new you" will be entering a whole new world in which love has many aspects and variations. Love is involvement. Vital absorption in things you feel passionate about is a form of love. You can love such things as work, art, music, and social causes. They can be satisfying and fulfilling, but they will be available to you only when you are no longer buried in your memories and pain. It helps to remember this simple law of physics: "Two things cannot occupy the same space at the same time." You have to release the pain to make room for the pleasure.

Whether you have left and are by yourself or are still in your abusive relationship and are feeling very much alone, you will fare better when you no longer desperately *need* to be with a man.

FOUR STEPS TO REDUCING YOUR FEARFUL EMOTIONS

Pam hated, loathed, and abhorred her husband's verbal abuse. At the same time she was terrified at the prospect of breaking up with him and being alone. She was perfectly able to take care of herself but was convinced that if she left, life by herself would be dismal and no other man would ever love her or want her. After all, she and Craig hadn't had sex in years and he had told her that it was because she had grown older and heavier and wasn't "appealing" anymore.

If you are at all like this "trapped" woman—trapped not by your partner or by financial dependence, but by your horror of leaving him and being companionless—what can you do?

You can use the same REBT techniques to get rid of your irrational fears that you have been using to change your irrational beliefs because your fears are based on your beliefs. For example, if you have an irrational *fear* of being alone, it is probably based on the irrational *belief* that it would be awful—or intolerable—to be alone.

The following steps will help you deal with any fears you may have. They are similar to those you have learned before and will serve as a good review. We will use the fear of being alone as our example.

Step 1: *Let yourself get fully in touch with your anxious feelings.*

Do not in any way sweep your anxious feelings under the rug. Acknowledge them, feel them, realize their depths. See that, for the most part, they are quite normal feelings, and that although not everyone in your circumstances has them, millions of women do. You don't want to be alone, especially if you are in a social group where being with a partner is the norm. You are used to being with one man, perhaps for many years. You really want the companionship, the financial security, the sex, and the other advantages of being with him. Why shouldn't you miss having them? Why should you not be fearful that you might not ever have them again?

See that many of your fears are normal and quite healthy. Don't put yourself down for having them. Honestly acknowledge them. Let yourself really feel them. If you are fearful, you are just that. If you are exceptionally fearful, greatly panicked, you still are just that. Let yourself feel what you feel.

Step 2: *Look for the self-statements you use to create your feelings and take responsibility for them.*

You might be saying something like "I *must not* be alone because it would be so awful that I wouldn't be able to stand it." Listen to the things you are telling yourself. Take responsibility for them. Perhaps being abused has made you feel less sure of yourself and more frightened of lots of things—including being alone. All right, so your abuser has created an environment that fosters insecurity in you. Let's acknowledge that, and lay at his door the responsibility for his abuse.

But what about *your* part in creating your fears? *Your* part in what you say to yourself? *Your* part in creating your own insecurity? How are you contributing to your extreme fearfulness? In truth, might you still be afraid of being alone even if you had not been "weakened" by abuse? Perhaps you have always feared being alone. Be honest. Look for your self-statements—your part of the problem—over which you have control, no matter what your abuser says or does. He does not make you say "No one will ever love me." Look at and "own" the things you are telling yourself that scare you into paralysis and doom you to being a victim in your own life.

Step 3: *Look for the shoulds, oughts, musts, and demands you are adding to your preferences, and recognize them as unhealthy.*

The same unhealthy shoulds, oughts, musts, and demands that exaggerate and perpetuate your irrational beliefs also exaggerate and perpetuate your fears. When you make a demanding self-statement, such as "I *must not* be alone because it would be so awful that I wouldn't be able to stand it," you are giving yourself an unhealthy, frightening message. When you make a "preference" self-statement, you are giving yourself a healthy, reassuring message: "I would prefer it very much, that I not be alone, *but* it's not the end of the world if I am; *but* it's not awful and terrible; *but* it probably will be only temporary."

If you have preferences, and not demands, you have choices of how to react to your worst fears—about being alone or about anything else. You can handle preferences; you can manage to live with them. But demands will make your life miserable.

Look for your shoulds, oughts, musts, and demands. Don't give up. See how they cause your fears and recognize that without them you would probably not have these feelings.

Step 4: *Forcefully dispute your shoulds, oughts, musts, and demands, and come up with rational, self-helping answers, or effective new philosophies.*

Keep seeing both your rational and irrational beliefs and fears, disputing the irrational ones, and coming up with effective new philosophies.

(Old) Irrational Belief: "I *must not* be alone because it would be so *awful* that I wouldn't be able to *stand* it."

Disputing: "How does it follow that my being alone would be so awful that I wouldn't be able to stand it?"

Answer (Effective New Philosophy): "It doesn't follow that it would be so awful to be alone that I wouldn't be able to stand it. I just might find that being alone awhile isn't so bad. In fact, I may even *like* it. I may enjoy the peace and find that I like being by myself and concentrating on what I want and like to do. It would be nice for a change to find companionship with people who truly like me—and treat me as if they do. Although I would prefer to be with a partner, I will survive and can still be happy and enjoy many other aspects of my life. I certainly don't have to continue scaring myself about being alone."

Disputing: "What results will I get if I continue to hold on to my old irrational belief?" "Does this thought get me what I want?" "Does it help me feel the way I want to feel?"

Answer (Effective New Philosophy): "Continuing to hold on to my old irrational belief will make it more difficult for me to make a rational decision about whether to stay or leave. If I do leave, holding on to my old irrational belief will keep me feeling fearful and unhappy. It will never get me what I want or help me feel the way I want to feel."

Conclusion: "Because I now see that my old irrational belief is not logical, won't get me what I want, and is destructive to me, I will let go of it and replace it with a new rational belief."

(New) Rational Belief: "I might *prefer* to not be alone, but it would not be awful if I were, and I would be able to stand it. I might even like it."

Now that we have dealt with the fear of being alone, we are going to talk about the other two biggest fears of leaving—fears of change and of the unknown.

FEARS OF CHANGE AND OF THE UNKNOWN

Everyone admires someone who has the courage to give up the familiar and try something new—change careers in mid-life or move to a city where they don't know anyone, for example. But most people are largely creatures of habit. They like adventure and excitement but also feel comfortable with regular routines because they are known and have a rhythm of their own. Even routines that are not especially satisfying are difficult to change.

The more insecure people are, the more they need the stability of familiar patterns and to know what to expect. This is especially true of those in abusive relationships. Their relationships become a familiar routine that seems less painful than change and the unknown. No matter how bad the routine, it has a known amount of harshness that can be tolerated. The fear that making a change could lead to something much worse often keeps people stuck where they are. They believe: "The devil you don't know is more frightening than the devil you do know."

This was true of Kathy. To change her ways, and to risk trying out new ones, were exceptionally "dangerous" concepts to her. She had been so beaten down by her husband, Todd, that she couldn't follow through on any of the things she had learned that might improve her situation. She couldn't even bring herself to walk out of the room when he was abusing her; she was too afraid. She knew that something had to change, but every time she thought about dealing with Todd differently or daydreamed about leaving, her fears stopped her in her tracks. If she left things as they were, at least she knew what to expect.

How did Kathy get over her fear of change—and how can you? Oddly enough, by changing. Your fear about making changes in your relationship or in your life by leaving is like most other fears. When you are afraid to do something, what causes your fear is that you dream up terrible consequences, and then convince yourself that if any of these dangers came to pass you wouldn't be able to deal with them. Of course, there may be *real* dangers. If you ride a bicycle, for example, you could fall and get hurt. If you begin handling your partner differently, he could get angry. If you leave, you could be lonely or find another abusive partner. If you make these dangers loom bigger than life in your mind, you will be too afraid to ride a bicycle, too afraid to confront your partner, and too afraid to leave.

But being too afraid of change has dangers of its own. Your *not* bicycling, *not* confronting your partner, and *not* leaving only increases your fear. And the longer you wait, the harder it is to act. The answer is to force yourself to do what you fear, go through the discomfort, and see that you can somehow manage no matter what happens. Most "dangers" will be less than you imagined.

After all, assuming you don't think your partner will become physically violent, he can't do much more than he already has if you change the way you deal with him. He may yell louder. He may get angry and throw a tantrum, or he may throw silent daggers and give you the cold shoulder for who knows how long. But he will get worse whether you confront him or not.

Since the fear of change is really a fear of how well you can handle new situations and conditions, the best way to reduce your fear is to force yourself to change some things in your life. Your courage to do things you fear is like a muscle in your body; to grow stronger it needs to be exercised. You have to risk temporary discomfort to ultimately make yourself more comfortable.

So exercise your courage by doing activities you are afraid of doing. Think, really think, about what is likely to happen when you do them. Then think of the hidden dangers of *not* doing them: lethargy, continued anxiety, lack of growth and development. Think of whittling away your life by constant fear and inertia. Which is really the greatest evil, do-nothingness or taking some suitable risks?

Begin with small steps such as changing some of your routines. Take a different route to work or go to a new market. Then do some relatively minor things that you find uncomfortable: Talk to someone while you are standing in line, go to a meeting where you don't know anyone, or go to a movie or a restaurant by yourself. You will see that you not only live through these experiences but cope with them better than you thought you could. As you move on and try changing other things, you may make some mistakes but you will learn from them. In time, you will grow stronger and may even enjoy bringing new and different things into your life.

Kathy had great success beginning with small steps. She was afraid to change the way she was dealing with Todd and much too afraid to consider leaving. She learned in therapy that before confronting these big fears, she could exercise her courage by forcing herself to make some smaller, less threatening changes.

Because Kathy had almost always been uncomfortable talking to people she did not know, she decided to try changing the way she reacted to new people she encountered in her everyday life. She knew she would be nervous and wouldn't be able to think of what to say, so she planned her approach ahead of time. Then, instead of keeping to herself, as she usually did when standing in line at the bank or the market, she began talking to people: "The lines are so long today. Do you know if it's always this busy on Fridays?" "I love your hair. Do you mind telling me where you had it cut?" Kathy soon discovered how nice and friendly most people are, and she actually started enjoying the conversations.

Feeling more courageous, Kathy decided her next step would

be to get herself over being intimidated by people she believed were "better" than she was because of their education and status. She joined a women's group at her church and forced herself to volunteer to serve on a committee with several members who were just the type that usually brought out her insecurities.

At her first committee meeting she felt uncomfortable and didn't participate until nearly the end when she had to answer a question. She found out she "didn't die" and no one rebuked her. In fact, one of the women said, "Good point. I hadn't thought of that." At the next meeting, Kathy forced herself to ask a question and offer a comment. She was surprised that later the women asked for her opinion on other matters. After a few meetings she began to make friends, in spite of her old fears of rejection.

Being able to change her behavior and conquer her fear made Kathy feel strong enough to take an even bigger risk and make a bigger change in her life. She tried using her new people skills to get a better job. She was a receptionist and had few job skills. Although she went to several interviews for an administrative assistant job, she found that it was difficult to get one with her educational and vocational background. She took some night courses at a community college and tried again. She got several rejections, yet persisted. After a number of tries, she finally got an administrative assistant job. Kathy felt unsure of herself on the job at first, but she stayed and soon became comfortable.

Then, with her decreased fear of change and of trying out new situations, Kathy was able to confront Todd and tell him that if he kept verbally abusing her, she was not going to put up with it and was going to leave him. At first he was shocked into behaving better but soon fell back into his old ways, whereupon she left.

Although Kathy felt very uncomfortable in her radically changed situation, she didn't go back to Todd. Getting over her fear of making new female friends bolstered her courage to make new male friends. Within a few months she felt better and was on her way to a satisfying new life.

Afraid that he would lose her forever, Todd reverted to being as charming and loving as he had been when she first fell in love with him. He swore he had learned his lesson and had mended his abusive ways. Although it was tempting to return to him, Kathy knew better. She had seen several girlfriends return to verbally abusive partners under similar conditions only to have their partners start abusing them again. Kathy finally told Todd to stop calling her and before long, divorced him.

You may never really feel very comfortable with change or you may get used to it and like it. But either way, you can get over your horror of it, so you no longer feel stuck in bad situations. Every time you successfully experience dealing with change, you will grow stronger and less afraid. Seeing that you can handle it and that change often greatly improves your situation will give you the courage to take action.

This chapter has begun the process of breaking down the wall of fear that has kept you powerless—a wall made up of individual fears so tightly packed that you could hardly tell one from the other. Now that you can see the fears as separate, you can overcome them one by one.

Before you go on to the next chapter, dispute one of your own fears. You can use the example on page 151 as a guide. Then we will discuss another category of fears that haunt women's minds and help keep them in abusive relationships that they otherwise might leave.

Chapter 13

Quieting Other Fears That Haunt You

Even if you have started using REBT techniques and the saber rattling of your partner does not make you as anxious as it used to, you may still be telling yourself things that keep you churned up. Thoughts of leaving bring a whole new realm of possibilities for creating fear and anxiety.

Some of the most debilitating fears are the irrational ones that creep into your mind in quiet moments and bring with them disturbing vivid images—images of you in agony over having given up your "Prince Charming" or of him being wonderful and gloriously happy with another woman. These kinds of haunting fears can paralyze you into indecision about leaving. As we have said, if you are to make the right choice about staying or leaving, reason—rather than fears—must prevail. In this chapter we will help you stop these runaway imaginary scenarios from dictating your future.

FEAR THAT THE PAIN OF LEAVING WILL BE MORE THAN YOU CAN BEAR

The emotional and practical aspects of leaving an abusive partner can conjure up overwhelming dread. You may fear both the pain of *being* without your partner and of *making* it in the world without him.

Let's consider the emotional pain of being without your partner. No matter how abusive he may be at times, the mere thought of not having him at all can produce powerful visceral reactions, especially if you believe you still love him. Just giving up the fairy tale of what you thought your life together would be is enough to tighten your throat, knot your stomach, and make you weep with grief. You might think you wouldn't be able to endure the loss. But you would. Other people do—and so would you. How? By using your new REBT tools to take control of your thoughts and by reminding yourself that your rational decision to save yourself from a life of misery has to take precedence over your raging emotions and insecurities.

Marilyn is a good example of someone who was able to do this. She was in an abusive relationship and stayed for years because she was so afraid of the pain of leaving. Whenever she thought about doing so, she felt overwhelmed. Although every-one's story is somewhat different, Marilyn felt the same loneliness, the same pain from her husband's attacks, the same fear of what the next moment might bring, the same concern for her children's welfare, and the same fear of leaving and insecurity about money that you may be feeling. And she felt something else—a powerful emotional connection to her husband that she couldn't even imagine being able to break, and still survive.

Unlike some women in her situation, Marilyn had a powerful tool: REBT. As she followed REBT principles and used REBT techniques, she had a revelation and the fog began to lift. She learned that she was emotionally addicted to her husband. She also learned that her imagination had created every worst-case scenario possible, and she feared that she would face all of them at the same time. No wonder she felt overwhelmed.

But she did her homework. She disputed her fears and made her list of the advantages and disadvantages of leaving. She thought about the years of pain and looked into her future. Then, with a deep breath, she forced herself to take a blind leap of faith. Since her husband had refused to leave, she took the children and moved in with her parents. It seemed as if a part of her had been ripped away and her life had been turned upside down.

The first days were rough, crazy, different. She felt lost. She reminisced, she cried, and she wondered: "Did I make a mistake? How am I going to take care of us if I don't get enough alimony and child support? Will my children be all right? Who am I without him and what am I going to do with my life?"

Then unexpected things began to happen. She noticed that the children were talking and laughing: They weren't worried anymore about "what" was going to come through the front door at the end of the day. No one yelled at her. She didn't shake anymore. Before long she was spending less time reminiscing and crying, and more time making her new life work.

She found a job. She found an apartment for herself and the children. She found peace and quiet. She traded a big kitchen for trips to the local take-out. She traded fancy vacations filled with tennis and tears for summertime weekend afternoons at the beach. But she's in control now and knows that things will continue to get easier. Already, life is good.

FEAR THAT YOU WON'T BE ABLE TO STAND HIS BEING WITH SOMEONE ELSE

Even if you have been hurt to the core and have finally gotten to the point where you don't want your abusive partner anymore, you still may not be able to stand the thought of his being with someone else. It is astonishing how swiftly the memory of the pain you often feel when you are with him evaporates as soon as you imagine him as his "wonderful old self" in the arms of another woman.

Stacy had this problem. For three years she had a wonderful relationship with Eric. Their love for each other, their friendship, their sex life, their social life—everything was great. Once in a while he would get overly upset about something small, but she figured that anyone can have a bad day. Then he became moody. She excused it at first, thinking that he was probably working too hard.

When his business faced more competition and began to decline and Stacy started bringing in more money than he did, Eric radically changed. All that had been good before gradually went bad—except for the sex—and somehow he believed that Stacy was entirely at fault. He seemed depressed—angrily depressed—about his business problems, and he became cruelly critical of her. Rather than blame *himself* for *anything*, he blamed *her* for *everything*. The same things he had previously praised her for, he now criticized. The active social life that she had always arranged so enthusiastically, and that he had so enjoyed, he now blamed for taking him away from his work and increasing their expenses. And the intelligence and business savvy that had attracted him to her and which he had appreciated during their early years, he now resented. And on and on it went.

But Stacy wasn't sure the problem was only Eric's. Maybe she *didn't* take his business seriously enough, as he often complained. Maybe their social life *was* too time consuming and expensive. Maybe she shouldn't be telling him so much about how well things were going at work when he had so many business problems. Maybe this and maybe that.

Stacy hoped that if Eric's business improved, he would stop abusing her. But when it did, he didn't. In fact, his anger became worse. Regardless of what Stacy suggested, he refused to do anything about it—no therapy, no exercise, no nothing. There was only his ceaseless blaming of her, which seemed temporarily to make him feel better, as Stacy felt worse and worse. Maybe there was something physically wrong with him. Maybe he was jealous of her success and was deliberately trying to put her down. Maybe he didn't love her anymore. Maybe, maybe, maybe.

After talking to her best friend, Stacy realized that although she was not perfect, Eric was being unreasonable. One day she had had enough, and he knew it. After that, he became very nice—for a while. This on-again, off-again, back-and-forth pattern continued for several years. She had great sex—and outstanding verbal abuse.

When Stacy began therapy, she was in bad shape, but she quickly learned REBT techniques and used them with great success. Before long she was ready to take a stand. She decided to give Eric a few more months, insist that he get therapy, or she would leave him to his misery. But still he did not go for help, and after a while, enough was enough! She couldn't be happy with Eric, and she would probably be unhappy without him—but less unhappy. She had options. She would not put up with this kind of tension and unfair criticism at work. So she would not put up with it in their relationship, either.

As the date set for her leaving Eric got closer, Stacy had second thoughts. Grim thoughts. She began rehearsing in her head all sorts of gruesome possibilities for her, and great ones for Eric. Suppose, just suppose, he would find another woman right away, as he kept threatening to do. She imagined him deliriously happy with one of the other single women they knew—or with one he would surely meet once she had left him. Maybe his executive secretary, Danielle, who was devoted to his business and couldn't seem to do enough for him. Or maybe his old girlfriend, Patti, whom he had once almost married. Or one of their friends, like Elizabeth, who had lots of money. Eric would be grateful for that. Some of Stacy's imaginings were likely far more glorious than Eric's life—or anyone's—could ever be.

Women like Stacy often visualize their partner, no matter how abusive he is, finding happiness with another woman; a woman they actually know or one they just dream up. They agonize over what they will miss by not being with him, and they torture themselves over giving him the freedom to be wonderful to some other woman and to fulfill all her dreams. They worry that other people will believe there is something wrong with *them* when their ex-partner is blissfully happy with another woman.

Do you, too, have this tendency? Do you visualize eternal bliss for your abusive partner after you leave him and he meets someone else? Do you really believe that he will have learned from his mistakes with you and will be different with her? If so, you may feel compelled to stay with him—and to suffer. To counter this kind of panicked thinking, you have to recognize the nonsense you are telling yourself and set it straight.

1. *It is nonsense to think that your partner will be ecstatically happy in a wonderful relationship with someone else.*

Will your abuser really have eternal bliss with some other woman after you leave him? You may think so, and so may he—at first. But soon his pattern of fault finding and verbal abuse will inevitably creep into his relationship with her. He is only capable of limited happiness, due to the unresolved issues and deep well of anger that rule his life and pollute his relationships. No woman, no ten women, and no relationship on earth could make him lastingly and fully happy and at peace with himself.

His abuse is a sickness that follows him wherever he goes. He may think that you are the source of his problems and that they will leave when you leave. But soon he will wake up to find that the sickness that destroyed your relationship has remained behind with him and he has to deal with it once again. So forget his being ecstatically happy in a glorious life with someone else. He will still be struggling with his internal demons. His new relationship will be based on his same old distorted sense of love and will be undermined by his gut-wrenching mind games.

Let's suppose that, in spite of all odds, your partner actually finds happiness with another woman. Suppose she is ideally suited for him, and the rocks in his head match the holes in hers. Well, suppose he does and suppose you can't stand the thought of it. Would you have managed to be happy if you had stayed with him? Does the fact that *she* is happy in spite of his abuse mean that *you* would have somehow found happiness had you stayed? You were already with him and you weren't happy. That's why you left. You knew you deserved better. What counts is whether *you* can be happy with a life of abuse, not whether *she* can.

2. *It is nonsense to believe that your partner is going to think the new woman in his life is so wonderful that he will not abuse her.*

Might your abuser find the ideal woman for him if you leave him, and will she be so ideal that he won't abuse her? Yes and no. He might find a woman he thinks of as ideal, and while he is on his best behavior, they may be like two peas in a pod. But even if he at first manages to be nice to her, to charm her, it would be temporary. It would be only a matter of time until he turns on her, as he turned on you. His pattern of entangling a woman in his web before risking abusing her is set, and it is unlikely he will stop abusing unless he takes the steps necessary to change—the same steps he is refusing to take even though his refusal may cost him his relationship with you.

Even if your partner's new woman is more compliant than you are, does 110 percent of things his way, agrees with everything he says, and is beautiful, capable, intelligent, and more, he will abuse her as he is abusing you. No woman in the world can be good enough or perfect enough to satisfy an abuser for long, nor to keep him "happy."

3. *It is nonsense to think that the new woman in your partner's life will be gloriously happy with the man of her dreams—your "Prince Charming."*

Does your partner have his good points? Yes, he may even sometimes be as wonderful, charming, and loving as any woman ever dreamed of. Remember, though, his wonderfulness coexists with his abusiveness. His new partner may at first think that the man of her dreams has finally arrived. But in time he will find fault, behave irrationally, and act out his anger in much the same way with her that he does with you.

She may enjoy some of his good points—the same good points that keep you locked into your relationship with him and that you fear you will always dream of longingly. But she will also get all the bad ones—the bad ones that are making you miserable. He is a package deal, otherwise you wouldn't be thinking about leaving. Keep in mind that his new partner will inherit your old problems. She will be his next "victim," the new dumping ground for his abuse. She will be getting your reject, your leftovers.

Like you, she will grow tired of the emotional roller coaster ride and will have to find her way back to herself—and to sanity. And like you, she will have to make a decision either to leave, or to stay and work at limiting her suffering and creating her own peace.

4. *It is nonsense to believe there must be something wrong with you if your partner has a "wonderful" relationship with someone else—one that you somehow couldn't manage to have with him.*

Your partner's being with someone else doesn't mean that there is something wrong with you or that she is better than you. It means that she is where you once were—at the beginning of a relationship with him. He loves her, as he once loved you. He is happy being with her, as he was once happy being with you. And, in time, he will abuse her, as he abused you. Then, their relationship will no longer be so "wonderful," either. Abusers do what they do—abuse.

So maybe he wasn't satisfied with you. He wanted you to be different, to be better, to be more. But who put him in charge of setting the standard for who is okay and who is not? Does it make sense for you to judge yourself by his distorted perceptions?

You were not solely responsible for the state of your relation-ship with your partner. You tried everything you could think of to get it back on track. Even if you regret some of the things you said and did, and you don't want to repeat the same behavior in your next relationship, that doesn't mean there is something wrong with you for having reacted to abuse as you did. Being with your partner probably brought out the worst in you. But there is no use beating yourself up and putting yourself down for your past efforts. You did the best you could at the time. Nothing you could have done would have made it better. Only *he* could have made it better—by stopping his abuse.

In any event, it was inevitable that you would lose some of your compatibility because it was based on his need for someone to abuse and your vulnerability to being abused. When you were no longer willing to play your role, that part of your compatibility died. So he found someone else to play your old role.

The important thing is to learn by your experience what not to do, what not to accept, what traps not to fall into in the future—and to get on with your life! That is what matters—not what happens to your partner. By now your priorities and criteria will have changed, and you will never again put yourself in the position of being abused in your most intimate relationship.

FEAR OF NEVER BEING ABLE TO LOVE ANYONE ELSE THE WAY YOU HAVE LOVED HIM

You may believe your abusive partner is the one true love of your life and be certain you will never love that deeply again. Carol felt that way about Bill. From the moment they met, he had been her "knight in shining armor." He was tall, strong, smart, and seemed to know how to do almost everything. When he took her into his arms she felt loved and protected. Even now, in his good moments, she felt he was the only one for her. In his bad moments, he was so mean she couldn't believe he was the same person. But he was the only one she had loved this way. Suppose she could never—oh, never!—be in love like this again?

Carol was in a real dilemma. She hated Bill, really hated him, when he was on one of his tirades. But she loved him, really loved him the rest of the time. Every time he flew out of control, she decided not to stay another moment. But she couldn't bear the thought of being away from him and felt she couldn't ever replace him. So again and again she talked herself out of leaving.

If you are like Carol, and millions of other women, you may have reached the breaking point and be all set to leave, but just can't get yourself to do it. If so, you can use your disputing skills to have the following conversation with yourself:

"Yes, I really do love my partner more than I have ever loved any man before, and I don't know whether, for sure, I will love anyone like that again. But the kind of love I have for him is not a healthy love. Other people find love again. There is no reason I can't do it too. I'll have many opportunities in my new life to meet new people. It may be just a matter of time until I meet someone right for me. I know I am capable of loving deeply. And this time I will look for someone who is capable of loving me deeply, consistently, and in a healthy way. If by some chance I am unable to find someone else to love, I will be sad and disappointed, but it won't be the end of the world. I won't die from it. I can still have companionship and love from other people and I can still have an enjoyable life—an abuse-free enjoyable life!"

FEAR THAT HE NEEDS YOU AND CAN'T GET ALONG WITHOUT YOU

In spite of your partner's dishing out frequent abuse, you believe he needs you, couldn't take care of himself very well without you, and would be desperately lonely and perhaps seriously depressed if you weren't there. Each time you start to leave, he says he "can't live without you" and begs for another chance. So you stay because you feel guilty.

Inflicting guilt is a favorite weapon of abusers. Your partner will likely use any means of manipulation necessary to get you to stay. Because of his gigantic fear of being abandoned, he will plead, appear helpless and pathetic, and promise to never abuse you again. Or he may threaten you or do or say anything else that might keep you from leaving. Abusers are experts at getting their partners to stay. It's one of their specialties, and you play right into your partner's hands when you feel guilty and let your guilt influence your decisions.

Let's say that, by some chance, your partner really *can't* get along too well without you. Perhaps he *would* get depressed and fall apart without your help and encouragement—at first. But he would somehow survive. You can leave him and still be a good, responsible person. You can even feel sorry and regretful about his predicament—and *still* not feel guilty.

From his frame of reference, of course, you are wrong and bad. But it's *your* viewpoint that counts. Although it is wrong to steal from someone, is it wrong to call a police officer when someone steals from you? Don't you have rights, and aren't you entitled to protect yourself from evil? Surely the person who steals from you will have a sad story that makes you feel sorry for him. And he may be devastated if you have him arrested. But, the law says that even if you kill a thug who is threatening your life you have done so to save yourself, and you are not guilty. Doesn't this go, too, for "hurting" an abuser by leaving him to save yourself?

Maybe it still seems wrong to you to leave your partner if he is in real danger of depression or "can't live without you." But what about the greater wrong of allowing him to continually abuse you? Maybe you won't fall apart if you stay with him. Maybe you can even have some satisfaction in spite of his abuse. Maybe you are much stronger than he is and can take his abuse more than he can tolerate your leaving. No matter. His cruel treatment, even when only verbal, is evil, wrong, unethical, immoral, vile, unfair, and uncalled for. Your leaving him, whatever the result, is surely the lesser evil—and it is his fault that it became necessary. You have a moral, not to mention a self-protective, right to this choice.

Let your abusive partner be as self-pitying as he wants. Let him beg you to stay—that is his privilege. But it is *your* privilege and right to escape.

FEAR OF NOT HAVING ACTED SOON ENOUGH TO SAVE YOUR CHILDREN

It may be true that it would have been better if you had left sooner. Your children would have spent less time growing up in an abusive household. They would have spent less time being afraid and less time getting the wrong messages about what love, family, and relationships are all about.

It's too bad your children have suffered. It's too bad you weren't strong enough or clear thinking enough to leave, and that you weren't ready sooner. But you weren't. And there is no way to undo what happened. Although you may have known it would be better to leave, you couldn't bring yourself to do it. Or you might have had valid reasons for staying for the time being, such as needing time to train for a job. Either way, your children suffered. But the fact that they suffered and you didn't stop it doesn't make you a bad or worthless person.

You wanted to raise your children in a loving home, and you did everything you could to make it happen. You did your best to be there for your children and to protect them from your abusive partner. Wallowing in guilt and shame now will only compound the problem and do nothing to solve it. It will only keep you in pain and sap the strength you need to change your children's lives and your own.

The good news is that there are things you can do now that will help all of you. You can override your emotions, be honest about your situation, and make a rational decision about leaving. You can emotionally support your children, be alert to any problems they develop, and seek professional help for them, if necessary—all without blaming yourself and putting yourself down. You can learn why you got into an abusive relationship and why you stayed. And, if you leave, you can make sure that it never happens again. Then you can teach your children by example what healthy living and loving are all about.

So far we have discussed primarily the all-important cognitive or thinking techniques for getting past your fears and making yourself feel better and cope better with verbal abuse. In the next chapter you will learn about some other widely used REBT techniques that will make what you have already learned even more effective.

Chapter 14

Embracing Your New Philosophy With Feeling

Suppose you are doing all the right things—paying attention to what you say to yourself, disputing to find out if what you are saying is true and provable, and creating new rational beliefs that serve you better—and you are amazed and relieved to find some of your old irrational beliefs disappearing as your new assertive self-talk takes hold.

You may have found, however, that some of your beliefs are resistant to change, and you are not entirely convinced of all the new things you are telling yourself. For example, you might be saying "It wouldn't be so bad to be alone," but you panic at the thought anyway. You talk to yourself, yet sometimes you aren't listening. Well, yes, you are indeed listening—mainly to your weak, fearful self and to your abusive partner. Although you hear him and your fearful self all too clearly, you have difficulty hearing your new, strong, courageous rational self. As a result, you are not feeling as good as you might, and you are not consistently acting in your own best interest.

Don't despair! REBT anticipates—even expects—that this will happen. Cognitive or thinking techniques alone are sometimes not enough to conquer deep-seated beliefs and fears. That's why REBT teaches a wide variety of emotive and behavioral techniques. In fact, one reason it is so successful in helping people with their problems is that it is a multimodal form of therapy. Throughout the world, therapists and people using REBT by themselves rely on emotive and behavioral techniques to help uproot irrational beliefs and fears that stubbornly persist, even after much disputing.

The reason a combination of techniques can produce fast, lasting results is because your thinking, feelings, and behavior have a powerful influence on one another. Changing any one of them affects the other two. That is why attacking stubborn old irrational beliefs on all three fronts can be so effective.

This chapter describes several of the most popular emotive techniques and shows how to use them. You may like some better than others, and some may work better than others for particular beliefs and fears you find troublesome. We suggest you familiarize yourself with all the techniques. They can make the difference between succeeding and not succeeding in changing your perspective and your feelings. When you combine cognitive, emotive, and behavioral techniques, you increase your chances of achieving your goals of feeling better, dealing better with your abusive partner, and being in better control of your decisions and your life.

VIGOROUS RECORDED DISPUTING

Usually people learning to dispute think they are disputing logically and strongly when they aren't. They sound very different than they think they do. In fact, most people are not aware of how they really sound. That is why some politicians, actors, salesmen, and job applicants use tape recorders when they want to perfect their speeches, roles, or communication.

You, too, can benefit from listening to what you are saying and how you are saying it. You may be surprised, even shocked, at how weakly you are disputing at first and how much stronger you will do it with practice. In REBT, using a tape recorder to practice disputing is called Vigorous Recorded Disputing.

In the late 1970s, I (A.E.) created the technique Vigorous Recorded Disputing. Since then I have used it with hundreds of clients to help them give up their irrational beliefs and the disturbed feelings and actions that follow.

Vigorous Recorded Disputing worked wonders for Sondra. Her husband, Ronald, was frequently angry and verbally abusive.

He made big issues out of the normal activities of a busy household. He also accused her of many things, including being an uncaring wife, an inadequate sexual partner, and a bad mother to their two children, 3-year-old Mary and 7-year-old Jimmie. Because Jimmie was borderline hyperactive, he was often difficult to control. Ronald would go into a ten-minute tirade whenever Jimmie acted up, yelling at Sondra, "Why can't you control this kid? What kind of mother are you? You can't do anything right." When she tried to answer him, he wouldn't listen.

Sondra came to me for help because she was tense all the time, felt like a failure, and could no longer stand Ronald's yelling and accusations.

When I talked with her, it became apparent that she was doing the best she could to deal with an abusive husband, a difficult child, and a busy toddler. As much as Sondra believed she was sometimes being unfairly attacked, at other times she believed she deserved it. A part of her feared that maybe she really *was* the inadequate mother, uncaring wife, and inadequate sexual partner that her husband kept accusing her of being. At those times, she beat up on herself mercilessly.

In our therapy sessions, I kept reminding Sondra of these important points:

- Ronald's accusations were usually either unfounded or exaggerated, which is typical of abusive behavior.
- Even if his accusations had all been true, that would not mean she is a failure or a bad person, or that she *deserves* to be abused.
- She was inadvertently making his blaming worse by buying into it and blaming herself for not being perfect.

But Sondra still held on to her irrational beliefs.

- If she really were as good a wife and mother as she thinks she *should* be, Ronald would not be angry and critical.
- Because she sometimes made mistakes, he might be justified in yelling at her and blaming her.
- She could not *stand* the unfairness of Ronald's blaming her for things that she knew were not her fault.

- He *must* realize how unfairly and cruelly he was treating her at those times, and he *must* stop.

When I got her to dispute these old ideas she did so, but not convincingly. She much more convincingly kept telling herself that they were true. To make her aware of how weakly she was doing her disputing, I told her to use a tape recorder.

First, I had her record her main irrational beliefs. She was strong, very strong, in stating the case against herself and in awfulizing about the situation she was in, and how there was no way out of it.

Second, I had her record herself disputing her irrational beliefs and listen to the tape. She couldn't believe her ears. She sounded just like a meek little girl: "I don't have to believe what Ronald says and I don't deserve to be treated this way. Just because I make mistakes sometimes isn't a good enough reason for him to be mean to me. I want him to stop treating me this way but he doesn't have to…."

It didn't take much persuasion to get Sondra to redo her disputing. She heard how much better it was the second time. Then she taped it several more times until she finally, very strongly, came up with statements like these:

"Ronald's anger and biting criticisms are a result of his being abusive. They are *not* a result of anything I say or do or am! He is irrational when he's behaving abusively and I never, *never* have to believe what he says. I don't ever *ever* deserve such treatment, either! I strongly dislike Ronald's yelling at me and blaming me, but I definitely can stand it, no matter how untrue or unfair his words are! I have endured his behavior so far, and I'm still here— and I'm strong, strong, *stronger* than ever. I am worthy of respect—from him and from myself—regardless of my human shortcomings and mistakes. Even when I have not done something as well as I would have liked, I *positively refuse* to put myself down! I am *through* with that—no matter how poorly I do or what Ronald says. I may well have some limitations as a wife, mother, and person, but that only means I am a fallible human being. So what! So is everyone else. And even if I sometimes make serious mistakes, I will always accept myself as a worthy person. I *will*, I *will*!

"My days of helping other people abuse me are over! They are over *forever*! I *absolutely refuse* to join the 'put-down party' with people who criticize me cruelly or unfairly—including my own demeaning, screaming mother. She and Ronald come from the same mold. From this day forward I will fight for myself and for my children—no matter how mean and unfair Ronald is. No law of the universe says that he has to see how unfairly he treats me or that he has to stop. But that's okay. I can deal with it. I will *not* let him bully me. I will *not* take responsibility for his anger. And I will *not* let him ruin our lives! I *won't*, I *won't*, I *won't*!"

Sondra continued recording her disputing at home, listening to herself, and deciding how she could make it more forceful and more convincing. After several weeks, there was quite a change in her. She stopped cringing when Ronald went into his usual tirade and, whenever possible, she calmly walked out. When she couldn't get away, she paid little attention to his words but spoke firmly to herself, using her new healthy self-talk. She recognized that his anger was his problem, not hers. She also practiced giving herself unconditional self-acceptance—especially when she did not do something as well as she would have liked.

After a while, supported by her effective new philosophy and healthy self-talk, she became strong enough to confront Ronald. Without going into detail or making inflammatory accusations, she told him that his behavior was unacceptable and was harmful to her and the children. She made it clear that she would do whatever was necessary to protect herself and them. She said she would like to be able to keep the family together and asked whether he would be willing to come to therapy with her. He reacted in his usual manner: He yelled and carried on. Sondra walked out. The next day, she said it again. And the next day again. This time he agreed to think about it. She asked when he would have an answer. Angrily, he agreed to give her an answer the next day. He sulked. He fumed. But he agreed to go.

Sondra and Ronald have been in therapy for several months. Sondra is continuing her growth and Ronald is making some progress. Time will tell what the outcome will be. In the meantime, Sondra is no longer beating herself up. She has gained control of her emotions and her life.

You, too, can benefit from Vigorous Recorded Disputing if you have difficulty convincing yourself of any of your effective new philosophies. Begin by recording your irrational beliefs on tape for ten or fifteen minutes. Try to dispute them very carefully and vigorously and listen to the results you get. If you have a close friend you would feel comfortable asking, have her listen to the tape too. See if she thinks that your disputing and your answers to it are strong enough. If they seem weak or light, or you just don't believe them, make them stronger and repeat them again and again until you are convinced of them. You will be amazed at how healthy your self-talk will become using this technique.

ROLE-PLAYING
STANDING UP TO VERBAL ABUSE

J.L. Moreno was a psychiatrist who, in the 1920s, began to experiment with role-playing and other dramatic techniques of dealing with troublesome situations. REBT uses a special form of role-playing to help people deal with situations they are anxious about, and to work through their anxiety. So, if you are panicked or depressed when your partner scathingly abuses you, if you can hardly think of anything to say or do, if you tend to break down and cry under his attack, or if you lapse into explaining and defending yourself, role-playing can be invaluable to you.

Role-playing with a friend, relative, therapy group member, or a counselor or therapist is a safe way to practice taking control of your emotions and standing up to your abusive partner.

In the REBT kind of role-playing, you assume your own role as an abused person, and someone else takes the role of your abuser. When this person severely condemns you, instead of allowing yourself to be terribly upset and unable to think of what to do—as you usually are with your real partner—you stand your ground and deal with it the REBT way. In this safe environment, you quietly and firmly answer the person who is playing your abusive partner. You work on not scaring yourself about the accusations. You learn to *be* strong by *pretending* to be strong. You make it clear that you know what is happening and will not stand for it. You answer your role-playing partner's remarks as best you can by saying something like "*Stop* it!" "It's *not* okay to talk to me like that." "I'm *not* going to listen to this any more." "If you continue, I will leave the room."

After role-playing this difficult situation for a while, and doing your best to cope with it, the person who is role-playing with you gives you feedback: what you have done well, what you could have done better, how you might have handled certain parts of the situation differently. This person may suggest alternative statements you could use and actions you could take to help you say more appropriate things and take more suitable actions in real life. Then you do the role-playing again, and you continue repeating it until you reduce your fear and are able to think, feel, talk, and act more effectively.

Remember, with role-playing, *you* are in control. Therefore, if you become upset or frightened, you can interrupt the exercise to discover what you are telling yourself. For example, suppose the person who is playing your abuser exclaims, "How could you do that! You're an idiot! You never do anything right!"

Hearing this abuse, you might break into tears and automatically put *yourself* down. That's when you stop the role-playing and investigate what you are irrationally saying to yourself to make yourself so self-hating. You could be saying: "He's right! I *am* an idiot! I *should* have known that. It's true that I never do anything right—and I probably never will. I'm lucky he's still here. Who else would ever love me?" You look at the irrational beliefs you are using to create your misery and paralysis and, with the help of your role-playing partner, you dispute and answer them. Then you go back to role-playing.

If you do this kind of role-playing a number of times, and do it with partners who know about your situation and who can support you in it, you will find that in spite of your being abused, you will be able to think of what to say and do. When a situation similar to the role-playing actually occurs in your everyday life, you will be much more prepared to handle it.

REVERSE ROLE-PLAYING
STANDING UP TO YOUR OLD IRRATIONAL BELIEFS

Another excellent emotive technique is reverse role-playing. It is effective for disputing your irrational beliefs and your consequent self-defeating feelings and behaviors. Reverse role-playing is especially useful when the usual methods of disputing do not work or when they work only temporarily.

In reverse role-playing, you and your role-playing partner act out opposite sides of your disputing—your healthy and unhealthy self-talk. *You* play your *healthy* self and the other person plays your *unhealthy* self. The other person pretends to have one of your old irrational beliefs, and strongly holds it and refuses to give it up. You take the opposing role of disputing the irrational belief and do your best to talk your role-playing partner out of it. No matter how well you argue against the irrational belief, your role-playing partner tries to rigidly maintain it. You persist in your arguments, no matter how firmly your partner holds on to the irrational view. You keep doing it until you feel that you can really fight this view and make an inroad against it. As you convince your partner to give up the old irrational belief, you will be convincing yourself to give it up as well.

I (A.E.) have used reverse role-playing in my individual and group therapy for many years with great success. Paula, who was in one of my therapy groups, found this technique very helpful in dealing with her most paralyzing irrational beliefs. She was convinced that she could never live happily without her attractive, successful boyfriend, Brad, even though he was unloving and verbally abusive. She thought that because she did not have any professional training, she could never afford the lifestyle by herself that she had with him. Paula also believed that if she left him, his bright, well-educated friends, whom she enjoyed being with, would not want to see her anymore.

So, according to her view, if she lost Brad she would be deprived of a high standard of living, a circle of interesting friends, and a man whose looks she had adored since she had met him and moved in with him five years before at the age of nineteen. Her whole life, she thought, would then be a shambles, and there would be nothing she could do to make it satisfactory again. Paula felt hopelessly inept and stupid, just as Brad kept saying she was, and was sure that she would fall apart at the seams if he actually left her, as he kept threatening to do.

Paula tried to get at the root of her irrational beliefs and refute them, but they kept coming back to plague her. She was nothing without Brad. She absolutely could not get along financially without his help. She could not have any good friends if he was not there to make them and keep them. She was totally incapable of getting another boyfriend who would not soon find out how inept and stupid she was and, like Brad, become abusive. Her only chance for happiness in life was in somehow staying with Brad and being a dishrag for him. She had no other, absolutely no other, good alternatives.

On and on Paula went with these deadly ideas; and, if anything, became even more convinced of their absolute truth. They were so stubborn that nothing I nor her therapy group could do to interrupt and demolish them would work. She would, at best, give them up for a day or two—and then quickly switch back to rigidly holding them and to compulsively staying with Brad even though almost everyone she knew, including her close relatives, advised her to leave.

Finally, I suggested that Paula try reverse role-playing. Another member of her therapy group, Laura, pretended to be Paula and strongly and firmly adopted her defeatist ideas. Mimicking Paula's unhealthy self, Laura insisted that she could not leave her verbally abusive boyfriend because she really had no other choice. She would rather be miserable with him than even more miserable without him.

Laura did an excellent job of playing Paula, and held rigidly to Paula's crazy ideas and behaviors no matter how forcefully Paula (role-playing her healthy self) tried to talk Laura out of them. Paula tried again and again to talk Laura out of her "pretend" defeatist ideas. It was a first for Paula to be taking a position of strength and reason. The two women did this kind of reverse role-playing several times in group therapy, while the rest of the members of the group looked on and critiqued what they were doing. Then they met a few times outside of group to continue Laura's stubbornly holding on to Paula's irrationalities, and with Paula trying to forcefully talk her out of them.

Within several weeks they really made progress. The arguments Paula had been using with Laura finally worked their way into her own head. Paula realized that she had choices other than staying with Brad, that she was definitely worse off with him than she would be without him, that she could get along financially if she were on her own, that she didn't need Brad as a boyfriend no matter how good looking he was, and that she could find some interesting friends of her own if she left him and none of their present friends wanted to continue seeing her. Having convinced herself of these rational beliefs, Paula decided to leave Brad on a trial basis. She managed to get along so well in her own life that she never went back.

Reverse role-playing gives you an opportunity to practice using healthy self-talk to get rid of your irrational beliefs. It is particularly effective because you keep hearing your own voice giving you healthy, rational messages.

RATIONAL EMOTIVE IMAGERY

One of the best ways of overcoming your fears is to use Rational Emotive Imagery. This technique was invented by a psychiatrist, Maxie C. Maultsby, Jr., who studied at the Institute for Rational, Emotive, Behavior Therapy in New York in the late 1960s. The technique allows people to practice getting over their fears in a safe, non-threatening environment.

Rational Emotive Imagery provides an opportunity for you to practice being in control of your emotions instead of having your emotions control you. Then when you are abused, you won't feel as upset or as helpless.

To use Rational Emotive Imagery, imagine one of the worst sets of conditions that may happen to you—such as being alone and without financial support if you should leave your abusive partner. Vividly imagine yourself in this "terrible" situation. Allow yourself to experience the feelings you would under these circumstances, such as panic, depression, and self-pity. Then use your old unhealthy negative self-talk to make these feelings stronger. Make them as intense as you possibly can.

Because you created these extreme unhealthy negative feelings and were able to make them worse, you can change them to healthy negative feelings, such as sadness, disappointment, and frustration that will make you feel less upset. Make this change by concentrating on keeping the same "terrible" situation in your head while you change your self-talk from unhealthy to healthy. Strongly tell yourself rational coping statements such as: "Too bad this is occurring in my life, but I can handle it!" "It's really rough being alone and without financial support from my partner, but it would be much rougher if I continued to live with him." "This situation I'm imagining is really, really bad, and it certainly could happen. But I could still manage to do many things and enjoy my life. Besides, if I stay with him, I will be miserable anyway—and maybe sick."

Notice that when you changed your self-talk, your feelings also changed. Repeat the same process for ten, twenty, or thirty days, until you are convinced that the very frustrating situation you are imagining is not a holy horror, and that you can survive it and still be a relatively happy person. If you continue to do Rational Emotive Imagery in this manner for a while, you will tend to automatically change your awfulizing philosophy to a sensible one and will tend to react to the imagined situation—or one that actually does take place—in a healthy manner.

To show you how to use this method, consider the case of my (A.E.'s) client Julie. Her husband, Bob, was verbally abusive. Their relationship had been deteriorating for years and although they still had sex, they were just going through the motions. There was very little intimacy. Julie was getting sick frequently and had irritable bowel syndrome. Her doctor had told her that her physical problems were due to stress. Over time her symptoms had become worse and she was afraid of what might happen to her. Nonetheless, even though she did not love Bob as she once had, she was convinced that she needed to stay with him for practical reasons, including that he and her brother were in business together and both families were helping to support her elderly parents.

At first Julie's irrational belief that she couldn't help getting upset and making herself sick when her husband abused her was resistant to disputing. I then used Rational Emotive Imagery with Julie by getting her to imagine some of the very worst things that could happen to her. "Close your eyes and vividly imagine," I said to her, "that Bob keeps verbally abusing you, just as he has been doing for the past several years—only more viciously.

Nothing you can do will stop him. He calls you every name under the sun, criticizes you and blames you for everything. He will not admit any responsibility for his actions. He insists that he is upset only because of your weaknesses and stupidities. What is more, he tries to convince almost everyone that he's as pure as the driven snow, and that you're a pain in the neck nag who keeps driving him to distraction and making him miserable. Can you vividly imagine this? Can you see him becoming cruel and ceaselessly berating you?"

"Oh, I certainly can imagine that happening," Julie replied. "Vividly."

"Okay. How do you *feel* as you imagine it? How do you honestly *feel* in your gut and in your heart?"

"As if I've been beaten up. I feel nervous and shaky, very angry, and my stomach hurts."

"Good. Get in touch with those feelings, and make them even stronger. Feel severely beaten up, extremely anxious, furious, and really feel your stomach aching."

"Oh, I do. I really do. I'm so upset I can hardly stand it. I'm in a rage and my stomach is killing me."

"Fine. Let yourself feel what you feel. Don't check it. Feel as upset as you can be. And now, since you created your feelings, you can change them. I want you to do just that. Use self-talk to reduce your extreme anxiety and fury. Change them to the healthy, appropriate feelings of uneasiness and annoyance. You can do it. Tell me when you really accomplish this—when you, at least temporarily, feel only uneasy and annoyed, instead of extremely anxious and furious."

For the next two minutes, Julie worked on changing her feelings, and then told me that she had actually done so. "I feel a little nervous and irritated about what's happening," she said, "but I don't feel shaky and furious anymore. And guess what! My stomach feels a little better already."

"Good. I told you that you could do it. Now, what exactly did you do to change your feeling? How did you change it?"

"Well, I took a deep breath, thought about what was happening in my imagination, and then told myself, 'It's certainly bad. What's happening to me is exactly what I don't want to happen—to be yelled at, blamed for causing my abuse, and to be in physical pain. It's very frustrating and annoying. And I'll never like it. But it's not the end of the world.' "

"That's fine!" I said. "You did very well in changing your unhealthy feelings to healthy ones, at least for the moment."

"Yes, I guess I did. At first, I thought I couldn't change my feelings—since they were overwhelming. But I kept working at it, and finally did it."

"Great. Now what I want you to do is a training process, so that when faced with situations like the one you imagined, you will feel unsettled and annoyed instead of extremely anxious and furious. I want you to do the same Rational Emotive Imagery once every day, for the next thirty days. As you can see, it only takes a couple of minutes to do it. First, imagine one of the very worst things that could happen to you, just as I had you do today. Let yourself feel what you feel. Get in touch with it, really feel it. Exaggerate it. Then change your feelings with the same coping statements you used this time—and with several similar ones that will probably come to you. Feel your disturbed feelings and then work at changing them. Do you understand?"

"I do. It's a training process you say?"

"Yes. What normally happens is that as the days go by, and you keep changing your feelings, you will start training yourself to automatically feel healthy negative emotions when you imagine very bad things happening or when they actually do happen. After ten to twenty days you will realize that you can control your feelings and that you can get better at doing it. Will you do this daily, until your new thoughts and feelings become automatic?"

"Yes, I will."

"Just to be sure that you keep doing it—since many people get lazy after a while—let me give you another REBT technique that will help get you to continue using Rational Emotive Imagery. It's a reinforcement technique that is also helpful in getting you to actually do whatever other things you commit to."

REWARDS AND PUNISHMENTS

B.F. Skinner was a brilliant psychologist who advocated the use of reinforcements, or rewards, whenever you want to change your behavior, particularly to establish and maintain a constructive behavior. (I [A.E.] added punishments to the rewards, thus creating a new REBT technique.)

When you are rewarded for a new behavior, you tend to repeat it and hold on to it solidly. When you are not rewarded for it or are actually penalized for it, you tend to drop it. These principles of reinforcement affect a good part of our lives. We work, usually, because we get paid at the end of the week. We go to the grocery store because it provides us with food. We try to avoid fatty foods, even though they taste good, because they raise our cholesterol and make us gain weight.

These same principles can be used effectively when you want to change the thinking, feelings, or actions that keep you helpless in an abusive relationship. This reinforcement method can help you overcome inertia and procrastination that might otherwise prevent you from using your REBT techniques regularly.

Begin by making a list of several activities you find rewarding, such as having coffee in the morning, making personal telephone calls, or watching the news on television before you go to bed. Then list several of the hard things you have been avoiding, such as doing your disputing or using other REBT techniques, or standing up to your abusive partner. Allow yourself the pleasures or rewards only *after* you have done fifteen minutes of disputing or using some other REBT technique, or *after* you stand up to your partner.

Punishment, too, can be an effective reinforcement tool. People will often perform one task they don't want to do, such as their REBT techniques, if it helps them avoid a task they want to do even less, such as cleaning out their closets. For this technique to be effective, you must force yourself to follow through with the punishment if you haven't carried out your commitment.

Rewards and punishments have no miraculous power. They are, however, wonderful techniques for getting you started in your new healthy habits.

Let's see how I (A.E.) suggested Julie use reinforcement techniques to ensure that she would do her Rational Emotive Imagery every day. I began by asking her, "What do you like to do every day, that you find quite pleasant, and that you do very regularly just because you enjoy it?"

"Hmm...let me see. Well, listening to music," she said.

"Okay. For the next thirty days, listen to music only *after* you have done the Rational Emotive Imagery and changed your disturbed feelings to healthy ones. Make listening to music contingent upon your doing the imagery method. It will be your reward." Then I asked her, "What chore or task do you hate and normally avoid?"

"Well, cleaning my house. I often avoid doing that."

"All right. Every day for the next thirty days when bedtime arrives and you have not done any Rational Emotive Imagery, you give yourself a punishment of staying up for an hour and cleaning the house. Will you try that?"

"Okay, that sounds gruesome enough. I think I'll regularly do the Rational Emotive Imagery!"

"That's the idea."

Julie, as instructed, did Rational Emotive Imagery to reduce her anxiety and anger, using rewards and punishments when she needed to. After two weeks, she noticed a difference in her automatic response when Bob abused her. She felt less upset and her stomach didn't become as painful. Julie began to believe in her healthy self-talk and was able to more forcefully dispute her irrational beliefs. By the end of thirty days, even though Bob was not abusing her any less, she felt much less upset, and her stomach pain was greatly reduced.

You have just learned several emotive techniques that help you change long-standing, harmful behavior patterns. You have seen how role-playing and reverse role-playing can make it easier to face your abusive partner. You have learned how recording your disputing and hearing how you sound can help your new rational beliefs take hold. And you have witnessed the power of Rational Emotive Imagery. In the next chapter, we are going to teach you some invaluable behavioral techniques that complement and support the cognitive and emotive techniques you have learned.

Taking Action Against Feeling Bad

Your new emotive techniques will prove to be important weapons in your war against abuse. Behavioral techniques will also be powerful allies. In this chapter, we show you what you can do behaviorally—that is, how you can take action—to cope with and change some of your disturbed feelings, and replace them with feelings that are healthy and appropriate.

IN VIVO DESENSITIZATION #1
STAYING IN VERBALLY ABUSIVE SITUATIONS WITH PEOPLE WHO HAVE A NON-RECURRING ROLE IN YOUR LIFE

In the last chapter you learned that by role-playing, you could practice your disputing and get experience handling abusive situations in a "safe" environment. Wouldn't it be great to have a safe way to practice handling abusive situations as they come up in real life? That's exactly the purpose of In Vivo Desensitization. It allows you to practice confronting your fears in a non-threatening environment. In the case of verbal abuse, this means using your encounters with abusive people other than your partner to develop your coping skills.

The advantage of using this method is that it is much easier to learn these skills when the person dishing out the abuse is not as important to you as your partner. Less is at stake, their comments and poor treatment of you don't cut as deep, and you are not forced to spend as much time with them. The skills you develop will carry over into your relationship with your partner.

We are not attempting to get you to either like or accept these people's abusive behavior anymore than we are your abusive partner's behavior. But dealing with abusive people rather than avoiding them offers a good opportunity to learn how to handle them and yourself better.

When using In Vivo Desensitization, you work on not giving the abuse super-importance and awfulizing about it, but viewing it as highly undesirable. In time you will find it easier to recognize when you are being abused and to remain relatively untouched by these situations. Ultimately, of course, you can avoid these disagreeable people or have little to do with them. But when you cannot avoid contact, at least you will no longer get churned up— a nice side benefit.

The goal is to remain calm and deal with the abuse effectively. Before long, you will be able to make yourself very sorry and disappointed about it, which are healthy negative feelings, instead of making yourself feel the unhealthy feelings of anxiety, panic, depression, and rage.

Here's how to use In Vivo Desensitization. In your daily life you will undoubtedly run across numerous people—salespeople, service people, and others—who behave rudely, insultingly, and discountingly. When you begin to feel that familiar "vague discomfort," pay attention to it. Ask yourself immediately what is causing it. Recognize that you are being abused. This is an important process, because you are probably so used to being treated disrespectfully that you often do not realize until later— when you are feeling extremely upset and emotionally spent— that the abuse has taken place at all. Then you are frustrated that you allowed yourself to be treated so poorly.

Once you become aware that you are being abused, practice disputing your irrational thoughts about the situation and replace them with rational ones. When you are in a self-helping frame of mind, you will be able to rationally decide whether the situation warrants objecting to the poor treatment you are receiving. Here is how In Vivo Desensitization worked for an REBT client.

Kelly came to me (A.E.) because she was in a verbally abusive marriage and wanted to learn how to have more control over her emotions. When her husband was on one of his tirades, she would get so upset that she couldn't think of what to say or do. After

Kelly learned the basics of REBT disputing, I explained In Vivo Desensitization and suggested that she begin using it.

Her first opportunity came when she took her car in to have it repaired. Kelly tried to describe to the mechanic the sound her car had been making. He cut her off, telling her that he knew what he was doing. He didn't need her to tell him how to do his job. When she timidly suggested that it might help him find the problem if he knew when it was making the sound, he snapped at her, "Who's the mechanic, lady, *you* or *me!*"

Kelly got that familiar feeling in the pit of her stomach. She apologized and left her car with the mechanic. As her friend drove her to work she realized more and more how upset she was. Although she thought the mechanic had been rude, it didn't seem as if his treatment of her had been *that* bad. Maybe she was overreacting as her husband often said she was, but she couldn't stop thinking about what happened.

After a while she realized the mechanic had behaved rudely and disrespectfully. She had not been imagining it. But she did *not* realize that her old, automatic unhealthy self-talk had taken over anyway: "I *should have* realized the mechanic was insulting me when it first happened. He had *no right* to talk to me that way, and I was *stupid* not to have told him so. Why am I *always* doing this?"

Kelly was on her lunch break when she suddenly became aware of what she had been saying to herself. She replaced her unhealthy self-talk with healthy self-talk: "I know I heard what I heard. The mechanic was inexcusably more than rude. But his behavior cannot upset me unless I let it. And this I refuse to do. I also refuse to put myself down for not realizing sooner that I was being treated abusively." Then she remembered In Vivo Desensitization and decided to confront the mechanic to practice overcoming the fear and upset feelings she usually experienced when dealing with abusive people.

After work, as Kelly's friend was taking her back to the repair shop, Kelly practiced her new healthy self-talk: "The mechanic is being abusive and I would *prefer* that he not be. I am *not* going to upset myself over it but I am also not going to let him keep belittling me. I can stand up for myself, and I can use this experience to practice coping with abuse so I will be better able to deal with my husband. Then, next time, I can take my business elsewhere."

When they got to the repair shop, Kelly was nervous but determined. She was not going to let the mechanic upset her again. He told her he had checked out the car and there was no noise. "You probably imagined it. Anyhow, there's still a charge."

She asked if he tested the car while backing it up, as she had tried to suggest earlier. "I told you I tested it," he barked. She paused for a moment, her habitual timidity creeping up. Then, supported by her new healthy self talk, she summoned up her courage and said: "When I left the car I tried to tell you that I heard the noise only when I was backing up. I am not going to pay you unless you listen for the noise while backing up the car."

The mechanic started to protest. With her heart pounding, Kelly calmly but firmly repeated her statement. He grudgingly climbed into the car and started to back it up. She heard the familiar noise and said, "Did you hear that?" He snapped, "It wasn't there before. Okay, leave it. I'll fix it."

When Kelly jumped back into her friend's car she was shaky, but elated. She had done it! For the first time since she could remember, she had stayed calm enough to be able to think of what to say and to actually say it. She had taken control of the situation and it felt wonderful. She thought of all the times she had been too afraid to protect herself from her husband's and other people's words. She could see that even though it had been difficult to confront the mechanic, it was much easier than confronting her husband, and she vowed to continue practicing her new REBT exercise until she could deal with any verbally abusive situation without feeling afraid or upset.

IN VIVO DESENSITIZATION #2
STAYING IN VERBALLY ABUSIVE SITUATIONS WITH PEOPLE WHO HAVE A RECURRING ROLE IN YOUR LIFE

It is natural to want to avoid abusive people in your life. However, as you learned in the last section, it is helpful to stay around them temporarily to practice coping with verbal abuse. We suggested that you begin with difficult people you come across briefly in your day-to-day activities. Once you find that you are able to handle these situations better, you can choose to take the next step: practicing with abusive people who have a recurring role in your life, such as relatives, friends, and co-workers.

Kelly, whom we talked about in the last section, had nothing to lose by confronting the mechanic because she could easily have her car fixed elsewhere and not ever see him again. However, when the abusive person is a relative, friend, or co-worker, there may be valid reasons for not leaving the relationship, just as there may be with your abusive partner.

Practicing with abusive people who have a recurring role in your life accomplishes two things at once. First, it helps you learn to handle their abuse so that when you see them you are more in control of your emotions and less upset by their behavior. Second, it helps you develop the skill to deal with your partner's abuse. We are not suggesting you look for verbally abusive situations to cultivate, but that you deliberately stay in existing ones—even when they lead you to make yourself upset or angry—until you have worked on reducing these feelings.

Select one or more people to use for your In Vivo Desensitization practice sessions. Co-workers are good choices because you are with them almost every day. Family members are good choices, too, because your relationship with them in some ways resembles the one you have with your abusive partner. With family members, expectations are higher and anger may have been building up for years, yet people are generally less willing to end the relationship.

Once you have chosen someone to use for your exercise, begin looking at the absolute shoulds, oughts, musts, and demands you are using to upset yourself about that person's behavior. For example, "My mother (father, sister, brother, co-worker) absolutely *must not* talk to me this way." Then dispute your absolutistic thinking and change it to preferential thinking. When you replace your unhealthy self-talk with healthy self-talk, it will reduce your upset feelings.

When you are no longer drowning in your own emotions, you will be able to rationally decide whether these relationships are worth continuing. Sometimes you will decide to remain in them for a number of good reasons, and sometimes you will decide that despite the good reasons, it is not worth it. Either way, once you have experienced changing your feelings with other people, you will feel more confident dealing with your abusive partner.

You will still dislike your partner's and other people's abusive behavior, but you will be able to stubbornly refuse to rile yourself up about it and make yourself absolutely miserable. When they treat you abusively, you can confront them. If that doesn't work, then decide whether or not to continue the relationship.

A Word of Caution:

Sometimes fears can be very helpful. They may be warning signs of potential danger. If you have any reason to think that the person you have selected for a practice session may cause you any harm, your fear is appropriate. Do not use either of the In Vivo Desensitization exercises to desensitize yourself to a valid fear or to practice with anyone you think might become violent.

SKILL TRAINING METHODS

Literally millions of women who are verbally abused are unable to fend for themselves. They unknowingly communicate to their partners the message that they can't leave because they will not be able to get along on their own. ("I need you. No matter what you do to me, I could never leave.") The fact, unfortunately, is that it's often true. This is one of the main reasons women stay even though they are unhappy.

Lack of assertiveness and the inability to cope with life situations would weaken anyone. They are particularly destructive for abused women. No matter how much some of them yearn to leave, to protect themselves and their children from the anxiety, fear, and anger, they believe they can't. They feel helpless because they are unprepared to assume full responsibility for their lives.

If you are one of these women, the mere thought of having to financially support yourself and your children may seem overwhelming. Maybe you were married young, had children, and never worked. Maybe you have been out of the work force for a number of years, or you may be working but don't make enough money to live on your own.

You also may have gaping holes in your knowledge of how to perform practical, everyday tasks—from programming the VCR to knowing when to have your car oil changed, from repairing the broken screen door to managing your family finances. You may have found it easier to let your partner do these tasks for you. Or, with a strong, controlling man in the house, perhaps you haven't been allowed the opportunity to learn how to do some of these things. You may even have been told that you wouldn't be good at them. Regardless, you have paid a price for not knowing how to do them—helplessness.

Self-sufficiency is a great equalizer of power in relationships. The more self-sufficient you are, the riskier it is for your partner to abuse you. And the only way you can make a free choice about whether you want to stay or leave your abusive partner is to know you can manage on your own. If you decide to stay, being self-sufficient makes you stronger and less controllable. If you decide to leave, it makes your life infinitely easier.

It is never too late to become self-sufficient. Neither being unable to support yourself nor a lack of knowledge of how to perform everyday tasks need to keep you from becoming independent. Just because you do not know how to do something doesn't mean you are not capable of doing it. It only means you haven't yet learned. In fact, when you attempt new things you may find—to your great surprise—that you can accomplish more than you ever thought possible. You may discover that you are handy around the house and are good at working on electronic and mechanical items.

Even if you have been a homemaker for years and are apprehensive about getting a job or returning to school to learn a new occupation, you can easily broaden your exposure to the world outside your home by beginning with a small step, such as volunteering at a school, hospital, or senior center. Soon you will feel comfortable in your new role as a person separate from your partner, and learning to become financially independent will seem less frightening.

If you are afraid of not having the time, energy, or ability to learn needed skills, or of being unable to juggle all the responsibilities necessary to be self-sufficient, remember that REBT is always there for you. When you use your new REBT skills regularly, you will no longer be wasting valuable time and energy on useless worrying, analyzing, obsessing, and beating yourself up. You will be better able to channel your efforts into positive, productive goals. And, once you are calmer and thinking constructively, you will be amazed at how much you will be able to do and how well you will be able to do it.

Begin by making an inventory of the skills you would require in order to be independent. Determine which are crucial and which have some importance but can be learned later. Choose the crucial skills you want to learn first. For example, your first priority may be learning how to maintain your house and car, or how to be more assertive. It may be learning how to handle your family finances or how to financially support yourself.

Whatever skills you decide to learn, help is plentiful and readily available. You can discuss your needs with friends and ask for suggestions. There are self-help groups that deal with a variety of issues. You can get professional therapy or counseling. You can also get valuable information from the many excellent books available and from the informative articles that appear regularly in women's magazines and on the Internet. Subjects range from working on personal growth to reentering the work force. Most high schools offer adult education classes. Community colleges offer training courses. Specialized training centers offer various certification programs. The list goes on and on.

Your lack of skills for being an independent person is serious and is not to be ignored. But it is not insurmountable. With some thinking, planning, and doing you can become self-sufficient. Set one small goal at time. Take one small step at a time. Have faith in your own ability, and then act on that faith with determination and perseverance. Before you know it, you will feel the rush of excitement that naturally follows every time you do something you never dreamed you could.

I (A.E.) still remember the time I ran into a former REBT client I used to call the "not me queen." When I had first told her that she could learn to feel less upset about being verbally abused, she said, "Maybe some people can, but *not me*." When I had first told her that she could learn to be strong and independent she said, "Maybe some people can, but *not me*." And when I had first told her that she could be happy without a man, she said, "No way! Not a chance. Maybe some people can, but definitely *not me!*"

She looked like a different person as she raced toward me. "Dr. Ellis! Dr. Ellis! Remember me? The 'not me queen'? Well, I mean I *was* the 'not me queen'—at least that's what you used to call me. But I'm not her anymore. You were right about everything! The abuse, my feelings, being independent—even being happy without a man. Can you believe it? *My* being happy without a man! I can hardly believe it myself.

"I found out I can do all kinds of things I thought I couldn't. I do little repairs around the house and I can work my VCR—*me,* the all-time least handiest person ever. I know when to change the oil in my car and I go to movies by myself sometimes. I even took a trip to Cancun alone last month—well sort of alone, Club Med, you know. I wasn't sure that I could do it, but I pushed myself to go and had a great time! It was a relief not to have you-know-who there to spoil it for me. And guess what! You were right about my being able to support myself, too. I took some computer classes and got a job I love working at an employment agency. I meet interesting people and I've made some new friends. I gave myself a new name, too—the 'can do queen.' I figured I've earned it. Isn't that incredible—*me* of all people!"

You, too, can become a "can do queen" even if you have been saying "not me" through most of this book.

RELAXATION METHODS

Being in an abusive relationship can keep you in state of constant tension that makes it difficult to ever relax. Cutting through the flurry of thoughts and tight, aching muscles becomes a priority.

For thousands of years, people who are highly agitated have used relaxation methods, such as yoga or breathing exercises, to train their mind and body to calm down. These tend to work, and to work almost immediately, because they interrupt anxiety-creating thoughts and make it almost impossible to focus on them. They work best when used on a regular basis, not just when you are upset. So establish a routine and stick to it. The physical and emotional rewards will be well worth the time and effort you invest.

There are many relaxation methods to choose from. Some may appeal to you more than others. You may already be familiar with methods you like, or you may want to try a few of the simple ones presented here.

Once calmer, you will be better able to focus on effectively disputing your awfulizing beliefs—and, at last, you will begin to hear your strong, courageous, rational self that will reduce your fears and anxieties and guide you to acting in your own best interest.

Breathing Exercises

One of the simplest and most automatic things you do is also one of the most "in the moment" practical techniques you can use to calm yourself. It's as simple as breathing. In fact, it *is* breathing. When done mindfully, it sets in motion a process of relaxation that can reduce your anxiety and fear.

How many times have you heard that when you are upset you should take a deep breath? It is said because it works. Although there are many different techniques, most are based on deep, or diaphragmatic, breathing. These exercises can be done standing, sitting, or lying down. The breathing technique is similar for all three.

Standing and sitting positions are good for "emergency" situations almost anytime and anywhere. Begin by standing or sitting tall and focusing on your breathing. Inhale slowly and deeply, lifting your ribcage and expanding your abdomen. Hold your breath for a few seconds, and then slowly exhale through your mouth, releasing all the tension from your body with your breath. You can check to see if you are doing it correctly by placing your hand on your abdomen and noticing whether it expands when you inhale and contracts when you exhale. Repeat this exercise several times or until you feel yourself calming down. Stop immediately if you start to feel lightheaded.

Doing deep breathing lying produces a more meditative relaxation response. Lie flat on the floor or a bed, bend your legs and let your knees fall together. Place your arms by your sides, palms up. Take a slow deep breath and feel your abdomen rise. Hold it for a few seconds. Then slowly exhale through your mouth, releasing the tension from your body. Feel your abdomen contract back toward your spine. Repeat several times.

If you practice deep breathing regularly, you will be able to rely on it when you are in the midst of an abusive incident and at other times when you feel particularly anxious. Deep breathing can quiet your racing thoughts long enough to help you deal better with almost any situation.

Progressive Relaxation

You may already be familiar with the well-known Progressive Relaxation technique developed by Edmund Jacobsen of Chicago University in the 1930s. Basically, the technique consists of tensing, then relaxing various muscle groups throughout the body in a specific order.

Progressive Relaxation increases body awareness. It allows you to recognize when you are carrying stress in your muscles and teaches you how to quickly release the tension. The technique also has a calming effect on your mind, since you focus on your body, rather than on worrisome thoughts. It is especially helpful if you are under chronic stress and being tense has become so "normal" that you have forgotten what it feels like to be relaxed—a condition common among abused people.

As you do the exercise, don't be concerned about following the exact order of the muscle sequence we give. As long as you move from your hands and arms, up to your head, and down the length of your body to your feet, tensing, holding, and relaxing the muscle groups as you go, the exercise will be effective.

Begin by getting into a comfortable position, either sitting or lying down, and close your eyes. Let any thoughts you may have drift through your mind and let them go.

Gradually make a tight fist with both hands. Hold the contractions for approximately ten seconds, paying attention to the tension building in your lower arms, hands, and fingers. Focus on the tension and describe to yourself what you feel—uncomfortable pulling sensations, burning, or tightness, for example.

Next, release the tension and let your hands and arms relax for approximately thirty seconds. Focus on the warm, heavy, relaxed feeling in your hands. Describe to yourself what you feel, and think about how it differs from when you were making a tight fist. Notice how the muscle relaxation progresses during the thirty seconds after you release the tension. You may want to try inhaling slowly during the tensing phase and exhaling as you begin relaxing the muscles.

After exercising your hands and lower arms, contract and release each of the following muscle groups in the following order: upper arms, forehead, eyes, nose, cheeks, mouth and jaw, neck, shoulders, chest, back, abdomen, buttocks, thighs, calves, ankles, and feet. (Some people prefer to follow the sequence first on one side of their body, then on the other, so they can compare the tense side to the relaxed side.)

As you progress through the muscle groups, you will feel a wonderful calmness gradually spread throughout your entire body. Your mind will become calmer as your thoughts slow down. Repeat the process several times or until your whole body feels warm and relaxed. Remember to pay attention to the tightness and pulling sensations when the muscles are tensed, and to the warm, heavy, relaxed feeling when they are released.

When you are finished, breathe in deeply and move your fingers and toes. Take another deep breath and stretch your body. Breathe deeply again and open your eyes.

At first, while you are learning, it is preferable to exercise each group of muscles separately, as we have described. Later, once you know the technique, you can exercise some of the muscle groups at the same time (your hands and lower and upper arms, for example). With practice, you should eventually be able to relax your entire body at once.

Meditation

Meditation is an ancient technique that is used by millions of people all over the world. If you have not experienced it, you might want to begin by listening to guided imagery audiotapes that take you through a relaxing mental and emotional experience. They can transport you to a beautiful mental place where your problems seem to drift away. There are also many other kinds of tapes, including those that sooth, help you sleep, heal your body, and fill your mind with positive thoughts.

Most meditation techniques are done without tapes. They seem simple, but don't be fooled: They can produce profound changes in you. Meditating is an inward journey that can calm you and change your worldview. It can also teach you a lot about yourself and provide a new avenue of personal growth.

One well-known form of meditation is Transcendental Meditation (TM). Experiments have shown that it leads to feelings of relaxation and ultimately provides a wide array of physical benefits, such as lowered blood pressure, release of physical tension and pain, and reduction of cardiac problems.

TM requires the use of a mantra, for instance, the well-known *om*. It is a word without meaning, but with a vibratory effect. It is recommended that a trained teacher select a personal mantra for new practitioners and teach them the meditation technique. However, many people who have read popular books on TM have learned the technique and chosen their own mantra. Once a mantra is selected, it is repeated again and again, blocking out mind chatter and inducing a feeling of peacefulness. If you are interested in learning more about TM, read one of the excellent books available or locate a training center in your area.

Dr. Herbert Benson, at Harvard Thorndike Memorial Laboratory, devised a method of meditation that he calls the Relaxation Response. It has become very popular because it is simple and effective.

To begin, sit in a comfortable position, close your eyes, and breathe slowly and naturally in and out. Relax all your muscles, beginning at your feet and progressing up to your face.

Now become aware of your breathing. Inhale through your nose. As you exhale, say the word *one* silently to yourself. (Or you may use another word, such as *peace*.) Repeat *one* to yourself each time you exhale. Inhale...exhale and say *one*. If any thoughts intrude, let them go and they will fade away.

When you finish, sit quietly for several minutes. Use this technique for ten to twenty minutes, once or twice a day. (Do not use the Relaxation Response within two hours after any meal.)

There are also other forms of meditation that may appeal to you. Take the time to learn about them. Explore and experiment until you find a technique you are comfortable with. Then get into the habit of finding a few minutes to meditate daily.

Yoga

Yoga is another immensely helpful ancient technique. It is particularly beneficial because it distracts your overreactive mind by requiring you to focus on both your body and your breathing. As you concentrate on the slow, gentle, complicated movements, you will find they fully occupy your mind, quieting your agitated thinking. As you slow down your body, you also slow down your mind, quickly bringing on an unusual kind of peacefulness. Although yoga exercises may not permanently calm you, they give you twenty minutes or more of rest. People who do yoga regularly find that they develop a "yoga state of mind" and are better able to return to that peaceful state when life becomes complicated. You can learn yoga by taking classes or from any of the many books or videotapes that are available.

Music

Listening to music is also a wonderful way to induce a feeling of relaxation and well-being. Find music that resonates within you in a special way and treat yourself to it often. It can be a form of self-therapy. It helps calm you down when you are anxious and helps pick you up when you are depressed. Getting absorbed in the music can change your painful emotional state and ease the tension in your body. Music is especially useful for interrupting obsessive thoughts. It is much better to listen to music than to a mind run amok.

Exercise

Many types of exercise in addition to yoga will do wonders for your mind and body. If you are not already exercising regularly, we highly recommend you begin now. Even a few times a week will make a big difference in the way you feel. Choose one or more activities you think you might enjoy. Get your doctor's okay first if you have any physical problems that need to be considered.

Begin slowly. Don't overdo. If you don't enjoy one activity, try another.

Aerobic exercise, weight training, toning, and stretching can all have a positive effect. Whether you take a daily walk or run, weight train, take aerobic classes at a health club or gym, or follow exercise videotapes in your own bedroom, you will feel better physically and mentally. Physical activity as diverse as martial arts training, Tai Chi, kickboxing, and dancing can be both fun and beneficial.

Exercise has both short-term and long-term benefits. It temporarily diverts your focus away from your problems and your negative mind chatter. It helps reduce your overall stress level and increases your body's natural production of substances like endorphins, which give you a feeling of well-being. It strengthens your body and helps you to stay healthier—and thinner!

Now you know there is much you can do for yourself, if only you will. You can practice dealing with abuse on "safe" people. You can develop skills that give you choices. You can mediate, exercise, and listen to music to reduce your tension—and so much more. Doing positive things for yourself is one of the ways of becoming your own best friend. Try some of the behavioral activities we have recommended. Find those that help you most and promise yourself that you will use them. Make it a gift from you, to you. You deserve to feel better, and only you can make it happen.

PART V

Living Happily
Ever After

Chapter 16

Taking Back Your Life

At the beginning of this book you were invited to embark on a new path to emotional freedom. You have learned a lot since then about your relationship, your partner, your emotions, your behavior, and yourself. You now know how you got onto the emotional roller coaster and what to do to get off. But to achieve true freedom—whether you stay or leave—you also have to take action that will help you regain control of your life. You have to grow out your clipped wings and fly free. Clear away the clutter of your addiction to your partner and explore the wonder of you and the magic of life.

This extraordinary state probably seems remote to you right now, if possible at all. But you have the power to achieve it. And you *will*, if you make it your goal and keep taking baby steps, one by one, until you reach it.

LIVING AS AN ADULT

Taking back your life begins with learning to live as a full-fledged adult—a separate, independently thinking, self-reliant whole person—rather than an intimidated child. This requires you to make fearless, rational decisions about the best way to handle your situation. You may decide to stay with your partner or to leave him. If you stay, you may decide to confront him about his abuse or not to. Regardless, you will be in charge of yourself, your emotions, and your life. Your options are many. Let reason, not habit or comfort, be your guide.

Take yourself in hand and do what you know is good for you,

even if it feels uncomfortable, even if you have to force yourself. That may mean asking your partner for change and requesting that he seek professional help with you. It may mean creating personal boundaries by setting limits on the behavior you tolerate from him and others. It may mean taking control of personal decisions your partner has been making for you, such as how you spend your time and with whom, where you direct your energy, how you dress or spend your money. It may mean not acting on your fear of setting him off: not leaving family gatherings, or other places, earlier than you want to; not turning down invitations to have dinner with co-workers; not anxiously keeping the house clean and the children quiet just to avoid trouble.

When you run your life out of fear of "stirring things up" with your partner or to avoid the "hassle" of going against his wishes, you are paying emotional blackmail. The cost is something more precious than money—your self-respect. And when you live your life as a prisoner because of your fear of his reactions, you also forfeit your dignity, your peace of mind, your growth as an individual, your right to be who you are and to choose for yourself how you will spend every precious moment.

TIRED OF BEING STEPPED ON?
GET UP OFF THE FLOOR!

You can take back your life quietly, with strength. And when you do, you may actually be able to initiate change. You don't have to immediately defy your partner and do something outrageous. You can begin in small ways. Do some things on your own. Enroll in a class you have wanted to attend that your partner objected to or go to a movie you have wanted to see that he doesn't. And take control of how, where, when, and with whom you spend your time. If you want to remain on the telephone when your partner says you have been talking long enough, do it. If you would like to see a friend he doesn't like, do it. At first he might become angry, but he is often angry anyway. Do what *you* believe is right for you rather than what your *partner* says is right for you.

If you decide that there are valid reasons for not going against your partner's wishes or confronting him right now, recognize that you are being oppressed by choice. Know that you are still in charge of how much you will stand for and that you can draw the line wherever and whenever you wish. You are not helpless and suffering is not inevitable. Remember, you have control over your reaction. You can recognize abuse for what it is, remain calm and clearheaded, and make a rational decision in each situation about how to deal with it.

IF YOU DECIDE TO SPEAK UP

If you decide to confront your partner, the next time he behaves abusively, look straight into his eyes, speak firmly, and tell him that you know what he is doing and you will not stand for it, will not participate in it, and will not let it upset you as it has in the past. Be brief. Do not allow yourself to get pulled into an argument. (Preparing yourself by using Rational Emotive Imagery, In Vivo Desensitization, and role-playing will make doing this—and doing it well—much easier.)

If he continues to behave abusively after you confront him, get away by going for a walk or visiting a friend, or by going into another room and reading or watching television. If you are away from home when you confront him, you can get away by going to the ladies room for a while or taking a cab home. (Always carry emergency money.)

If you are on the telephone with your partner and he speaks abusively to you, tell him firmly that you refuse to listen when he is being abusive and that unless he stops immediately you are going to hang up. If he continues, then do it.

Speaking up, walking out, and hanging up are powerful ways of setting limits on your partner's treatment of you.

BREAKING FREE AND RECLAIMING YOURSELF AND YOUR LIFE

When you stop participating in the abuse, react rationally, and manage your emotions the REBT way—whether or not you confront your partner—you will witness a most interesting scene: him doing his nutty, irrational, angry, spoiled, self-centered, demanding child routine, all by himself. You will have taken control, your self-respect will soar, and the balance of power will begin to shift. The stronger and more resolute you are, the sooner it will happen. Remember, you have as much power as you choose to have. Your partner's only control is that which you have given him. And just as you have given it to him, you can take it back. Intimidation is your jailer. But you can break free. Make up your mind to reclaim your self and your life—and do it!

Pour some of your newfound energy into finding out who you are, what happened to your dreams, what makes your heart sing. Make every day a celebration of you. Do something for yourself and thank yourself for it. Honor your feelings, always. Be patient, kind, and gentle with yourself. You are like a small child taking her first steps. Encourage yourself, hug yourself, give yourself a compliment, tell yourself what a good job you are doing. Feel your power, live your freedom—and you will begin to heal.

SOME IMPORTANT WORDS THAT CAN SAVE YOUR LIFE

If you suspect that your partner might become violent if you go against his wishes or stand up to him, don't do it without professional help. But don't fool yourself into believing that as long as you continue doing as he wants and you do not confront him, you are safe. Remember, verbal abusers react to their internal turmoil, and most anything can trigger a physical attack in an abuser who is prone to violence. Insults that wrap themselves around your psyche can, in an instant, become fingers that wrap themselves around your neck. The danger is real.

Believing that your partner is incapable of such behavior will not save you from his attacks should they occur. You must get professional help, develop a temporary emergency plan for leaving in a hurry should you need to, and seriously consider leaving your partner permanently before he becomes violent. Your life may depend on it.

If you don't think your partner will become violent, you still need to proceed cautiously when going against his wishes or standing up to him. He may become angry—perhaps very angry—when you change your behavior, and you must assess the degree of his anger for your own safety. While most verbal abusers never become physically abusive, some do. All physically abusive partners verbally abused first. There is no sure way to tell whether your partner is one of those who will become violent.

If when you confront your partner he ever threatens to harm you or blocks you from leaving or breaks or throws things or slams his fist into a wall or door, or if the veins on his neck stand out and he seems to be forcing himself to hold back his anger, immediately stop trying to deal with the abuse by yourself, get away from him, and get professional help. These are warning signs that a physical attack may be imminent.

Do what you know is right for you by enlisting the help you need to take back your life safely. Don't make excuses for your partner or delude yourself into thinking that everything will be all right. Think rationally rather than emotionally. Do what you would advise a friend to do if she were in your situation.

YOU CAN LIVE HAPPILY EVER AFTER

Regardless of the severity of your situation remember that REBT is there to help you. Actively and regularly use REBT principles, techniques, and philosophy to deal with your abuse, and their remarkable positive effects will reach out and embrace every issue, every problem, every situation that comes to you. Neither you nor your life will ever be the same. Accepting REBT as the foundation of your life will make every step toward emotional freedom infinitely easier. And it will make you better able to cope with anything that comes your way.

Now you know the secret of overcoming verbal abuse, and you know that what we told you at the beginning of this book about your being able to live happily ever after, after all, is true. It is all up to you.

We leave you with this guiding thought from Robert Louis Stevenson: "To be what we are, and to become what we are capable of becoming, is the only end of life."

Chapter 17

A Personal Word From Marcia Grad Powers

As you finish reading this book and close it, you are also closing the door on a chapter of your life. The fog of confusion and isolation has lifted. Even though the abuse will likely march on if you stay in your relationship, your new understanding of it and new tools for dealing with it will change your experience of it. And when you sometimes slip back into old ways of thinking and behaving, it will seem different. Why? Because the door has slammed shut on ignorance. You know what you know. There is no going back to not knowing, and no more hiding from the truth through denial.

What you *do*—or *don't* do—about your abuse is up to you; however, here is something crucial to keep in mind. It may seem as if the way you cope with your abuse and whether you decide to stay or leave affects only you and a small circle of your family and close friends. But that isn't true. What you do or don't do ultimately affects many more people than you ever imagined.

SOCIETY MIRRORS OUR LIVES AT HOME

As members of today's society, many of us have feelings of anger, frustration, and fear. We sometimes feel as if society is spinning out of control. Violent and white-collar crimes have become commonplace. A general lack of ethics, morals, manners, and personal responsibility is apparent everywhere; from a plethora of angry, aggressive drivers to an epidemic of lawsuits blaming others for our poor choices, lack of good judgment and common sense, and our foolish behaviors.

We ask ourselves what has happened? What has changed that renders us afraid to do the life-enhancing things we once did freely: smile at nearby drivers at stop signals; strike up conversations with people in public places; go for walks on our city streets; enjoy quiet moments in our local parks; visit convenience stores, use ATM machines, leave our cars in parking garages with confidence that it—and we—will be safe?

Our feelings of anxiety, confusion, lack of control, and helplessness about the society in which we now live, for many of us, mirror the feelings we experience in our families. Abuse is a major player in our societal woes, yet we perpetuate it by allowing it to continue in our own relationships. When we choose to not take individual responsibility for stopping our own abuse, we are helping to create a society we often dislike. If things are ever to get better, we must set a new standard of behavior.

STOPPING THE LEGACY OF ABUSE IS OUR CHILDREN'S ONLY HOPE

It is said that children are the hope of the future. In fact, *we* are the hope of the future; for without our teaching by example what healthy living and healthy loving are all about, our children will have difficulty attaining them.

Crime, violence, and children out of control; much of it begins with us—the mothers, grandmothers, teachers, and other role models for younger generations. We have been given tender young lives to shape and mold. Are we going to continue raising our children to become empty, angry, disempowered adults who take their frustrations out on their partners, their children, and on society?

Every day we are being emulated by children who believe that domination and subservience are acceptable and that it is "normal" to hurt and be hurt in the name of love. It is all some of them have ever experienced. Although reading about loving relationships, seeing them in movies and on television, and being with friends' loving families may show children that real love is possible and may influence some of them to strive for loving relationships in their own adult lives, many more follow in our footsteps and in those of their societal role models—top athletes and well-known actors—who make headlines with their dramatic abusive relationships and alcohol and drug addictions.

The proof of our influence is all around us. Abusive teenage "love" relationships are on the increase, as is teenage pregnancy; and younger and younger children are becoming abusive to each other and committing serious crimes. Programs to educate students about abuse are popping up in schools around the country but there are not enough of them, and although they can be extremely helpful, they have limited influence if students are returning to abusive households at the end of the school day.

There is not a woman among us who wants her children to live as she has lived—with anxiety, insecurity, powerlessness, fear, and anger. Yet we systematically teach them exactly that by trapping them in a home environment that produces these feelings. It is up to us to put a stop to this. It is our children's and society's only hope.

We have a responsibility to learn the universal truths that shape our lives—individually and collectively—to live by them and to teach them to our children, who look to us to see how to conduct their relationships and their lives. We must create a home environment in which our children will flourish and grow up to become self-respecting, law-abiding, moral, ethical, psychologically healthy, loving, fulfilled, happy human beings—human beings who know how to deal with their feelings and how to face life's adversities with strength, dignity, and a sense of personal responsibility. We must shout from our rooftops with conviction: "We refuse to allow our children to leave our homes as members of the 'walking wounded,' more comfortable with chaos than with calm, more used to love hurting than feeling good, and full of anger and pain that may play itself out on us, their partners, their children, and society."

FIND STRENGTH IN OUR NUMBERS AND IN OUR COLLECTIVE WISDOM

Verbal abuse is covert, hidden, and isolating. It causes us to feel alone in our pain; but in truth, we aren't. What seems to us—

especially in our darkest moments—to be a solitary struggle is actually a collective battle. We are each a part of an estimated millions-strong sisterhood of women who have shared the horrendous experience of abuse. Women who want to do more than survive and overcome. Women who want to grow stronger, prouder, and more courageous. Women who want to hold their heads high, and want to have the energy to do it. Women who want to focus on how good it *is*, rather than on how bad it *was*. Women who want to be in a romantic, respectful, fulfilling, supportive, enduring love relationship. Women who want to be happy, healthy, and fulfilled. Women who want to stop the legacy of abuse that millions of us are bequeathing our children.

There is great strength in our numbers. Strength in our collective knowledge of what works and what doesn't. Strength in our overwhelming desire to make it all count for something. Strength in our determination to stop our pain and show our children firsthand another way to live and love.

The time has come for those of us who have found our way, whose lives are full and peaceful and happy at last, to speak out and encourage others. We who have done it. We who have set ourselves emotionally free. If we can do it, so can you. Then you, too, can become a living example to women who may doubt their ability to cope with the debilitating situation they find themselves in. One day you, too, can have the satisfaction of speaking out to encourage and guide others. You, too, can set an example of healthy living and healthy relationships for our children. Every one of us who reclaims her personal power becomes a model of hope for others who don't know how or who are afraid to try.

Can we create the lives we want and change the course of society? Can we stop being downtrodden victims, settling for less than we deserve? Yes. We have done it before. Women banding together for worthy purposes have been a major societal force throughout history. Indeed we have *made* history by working hard for equality in the voting booth, in educational facilities, and in the workplace.

We have also in many ways changed the face of male, female relationships. We have achieved much, step by step. Yet millions of us who are verbally abused still face one of our biggest challenges ever: to let go of our fairy tale long enough to see and change the pattern of our love relationships. To stop being so paralyzed by the present that we can't see into the future. To do less sighing, crying, and conceding, and more taking charge of our emotions and our lives.

Together, in time, we can stop this insanity, this imprisonment of women's psyches and souls, and the systematic programming of so many of our children to repeat the cycle of abuse they are *brought* up in and *caught* up in. Each one of us who decides to save herself, helps to save us all. There is a saying: "Save one life and you save the world." We can help save each other and save our children by choosing to save ourselves. We can turn it all around, one person at a time. Every woman who succeeds makes us all stronger, more determined, and more convinced that we can do it—even under the worst circumstances.

Taking control of your emotions can literally transform your life, the lives of those you love, and the lives of many people you have never met. You can make a difference. You can do your part in initiating a major shift in consciousness. The ripple effect on good and bad is awesome. Just as one person touched by anger, fear, helplessness, and hopelessness becomes two, and two becomes four; so one person touched by courage, empowerment, serenity, and happiness becomes two, and two becomes four, and so on. Most life-changing societal movements begin with one or a few people. Change yourself and you will have done your part in changing the world.

YOU HAVE BEEN TRAPPED IN A PRISON OF YOUR OWN MAKING THOUGH THE DOOR TO FREEDOM STANDS WIDE OPEN BEFORE YOU

Walking through the door to freedom means that you become strong in your convictions about yourself—your intrinsic value, your deservedness of respect, love, happiness, and peace of mind. It means trusting yourself to know what is in your best interest, and consistently acting on that knowledge. Without these convictions, you relinquish it all too easily when a "Prince Charming" comes along and tries to take all away. You let him take from you the most precious treasures you own—your perceptions, your self-respect, your dignity, your belief in yourself. They are stolen by a chameleon to whom you hand over the weapons to subdue and overtake you.

Walking through the door to freedom simply requires that you be willing to put one foot in front of the other, doing whatever it takes to continue moving forward. It means learning how to insulate yourself from the emotional, psychological, and physical harm that can result from being in a verbally abusive relationship. It means recognizing that every battered woman who ends up in an emergency room was once being verbally abused but believed that her "Prince Charming" would never physically harm her.

You may think you haven't the strength or courage to walk through the door to freedom—but you would be wrong. It has taken great strength and courage to get to where you are now, and walking through that door with determination can help you find more strength and courage than you ever realized you had. Whether or not you can bring yourself to believe it right now, you are stronger than the circumstances you find yourself in.

What is on the freedom side of the door? All that you desire— healing, comfort, peace, self-respect, self-love, and personal power. Even so, you may be reluctant to go. You may fear the unknown demons you believe are lying in wait for you, or you may fear that the great unknown will swallow you up. Take heart. Many of us have felt as you do; yet we found that our fears of what *might* happen were far worse than what *did* happen.

You've been given a life to live. Don't wait to find yourself looking back someday, seeing only wasted years, unfulfilled dreams, and eroded health. This is a common lament of women who have allowed lack of knowledge or fear or denial to keep them stuck in emotional turmoil too long. Remember, sometimes you need to go with a commitment to yourself rather than with your feelings. Give this careful thought. Just because you *feel* something doesn't make it so. Reason must be allowed to overcome your desire for that which is bad for you.

Putting a commitment to themselves ahead of their unreliable feelings has helped many women go bravely forward—even though a frightened voice from within was screaming, "No, No, don't rock the boat!" *Rocking* the boat, however, is not the problem. The fact that you are on a *sinking* boat is the problem. So don't wait for it to "feel right" before you take action to improve or leave your situation. It may never "feel right." But it may be the best decision you ever made.

THINGS YOU CAN DO TO CONTINUE ON THE PATH TO EMOTIONAL FREEDOM

The purpose of this book has been to help you begin your journey to emotional freedom. Remember that you are not traveling alone; you have your new REBT tools to accompany you. Use them to keep the momentum going as you continue your exciting journey toward happiness and peace.

- Refer to this book every day until you are crystal clear about how your relationship works and until REBT techniques become second nature to you.
- Do your disputing and use other REBT techniques regularly.
- Keep your list of rational coping self-statements handy and refer to them frequently.
- Read *A Guide to Rational Living* by Drs. Albert Ellis and Robert A. Harper; *A Guide to Personal Happiness* by Albert Ellis, Ph.D. and Irving Becker, Ed.D.; *The Princess Who Believed in Fairy Tales* and *Charisma: How to get "that special magic,"* both by Marcia Grad. Reread them whenever you want to be inspired or guided back to healthy thinking and emotions. (See the catalog at the end of this book.)
- Increase your knowledge of REBT by reading the questions and answers at www.rebt.org, and by listening to audiotapes from the Albert Ellis Institute. For a catalog, call (800) 323-4738, fax (212) 249-3582, e-mail info@rebt.org, or go to www.rebt.org.
- Find an REBT therapist experienced in abuse issues. Contact the Albert Ellis Institute, 45 East 65th Street, New York, N.Y. 10021-6593. Phone: (212) 535-0822. Fax: (212) 249-3582. E-mail: info@rebt.org. Web site: www.rebt.org. Or call for referrals from organizations that provide help for abused women.

Here are some valuable tips from those of us who have traveled the path to emotional freedom before you:

- If you have been keeping your situation a secret, get it out in the open by confiding in someone who cares about you.
- Join a women's support or therapy group.
- Contact a women's center or family services center.
- Build a circle of friends and family members who understand what you are going through and encourage your personal growth.
- Build a supportive, gentle, loving relationship with yourself. Talk kindly to yourself. Give yourself a compliment every day. Acknowledge and praise yourself aloud. Remember that generally people will treat you the way you treat yourself.
- Remind yourself daily that your first priority is to take care of yourself.
- Find out who you are. Do whatever you can to experience your separateness from your partner. Develop your individuality. Pursue new interests by joining groups of like-minded people.
- Develop your abilities and learn skills that can help make you financially independent.
- In difficult moments, rely on this magic question: "What would Dr. Ellis say?"
- Live your new philosophy of life every day. "...I will love myself, be tender with myself, and fill my days with people who care and share. I will celebrate my uniqueness and my inner power. I will joyfully open my heart to the birds that sing, the stars that twinkle, and the flowers that bloom each spring."
- Spread the word to others. When you open up to other women, you will find that many are in situations hauntingly similar to your own. Be supportive of one another. We all feel saner when we realize someone understands and has felt what we are feeling. Share the knowledge and wisdom you have gleaned from your experience.

Remember, you are part of a sisterhood that can help women reclaim their minds, their souls, and their lives.

Whether or not you stay with your abusive partner, keeping your new rational beliefs uppermost in your mind will make day-to-day coping easier. Here are some reminders that will help you hold on to your beliefs:

- Verbal abuse is a form of violence. It is a form of brainwashing. It is a form of psychological and emotional torture. It is a form of control with mental anguish and emotional dependence. It is not a form of love. It is not "just the way your partner is."
- Abuse is never warranted, never deserved, and never justified.
- You do not cause the abuse. Your partner does.
- You could never be "good enough" to end the abuse.
- You cannot change him. He must do that himself.
- Your partner is not your friend. He is not trying to help you or teach you and is not interested in helping you feel better. He does not have your best interest at heart.
- You cannot reason with your partner when he is behaving irrationally. He will not understand your point of view, no matter how many different ways you attempt to explain.
- If you feel as if you are being attacked, you probably are.
- You do not have to get pulled into your partner's craziness. You have choices as to how you will react.
- Generally, abuse escalates unless your partner gets professional help and does all that is necessary to stop abusing.
- Crumbs of decent, caring, loving, normal behavior do not make a feast. Acknowledge the famine and do something about it.
- Exposing yourself to long-term verbal abuse puts you in jeopardy—emotionally, physically, and spiritually. Short of leaving, diffusing your toxic reaction is the best way to limit the potential toll it can take on you.

- Self-respect is like a muscle; the more you exercise it, the stronger it becomes.
- You are worthy of respect from others.
- You cannot expect other people to treat you any better than you treat yourself.
- The stronger and more independent you grow, and the more accepting of yourself you become, the more likely you will choose to do what is in your best interest.

FREE AT LAST
BEGINNING YOUR NEW LIFE

Whether you are staying, leaving, or have left, you can be emotionally free and see life anew. As a wise adage says, "Today is the first day of the rest of your life." It is never too late to find peace and happiness. It's an "inside job" that you can begin now.

Many of us who have been where you are now found it difficult to imagine that the pain would ever stop. Being happy was hardly a thought; it seemed so far away. We had believed that life was just a bowl of cherries—until one day we woke up and realized that someone had stolen all the cherries and left us with nothing but the pits. But we didn't settle for the pits indefinitely. We sowed fertile new fields in our minds and we grew and grew. Now the fruit of our lives is sweet.

How did we do it? By choosing to perceive our abuse as a learning tool and using it as a stepping-stone to a better life and a better understanding of ourselves. By determinedly taking back the personal power we had unknowingly given away. By learning to respect ourselves and knowing we are worthy of respect from others. By searching for balance, meaning, and purpose as well as true love.

If you are with us, if you want to do as we have done, take your dreams out of storage and dust them off, for your emotional rags to riches story is about to unfold.

Now, some powerful advice from Henry Herbert Hoot, D.H. (Doctor of the Heart) in *The Princess Who Believed in Fairy Tales*.

"Go forth and live your highest truth, Princess."

Etch these words into your mind. Take them into your heart. For if you live them, really live them, they will lift your spirit and transform your life.

May your path be filled with learning, love, and laughter—and may we someday meet again along the way.

From the Authors

Dear Reader,

We want you to be able to use the information you have learned from this book to make a real difference in your life. And we want to make future editions even more helpful. Therefore, we would appreciate your sharing the results you are getting as you integrate REBT principles and techniques into your life. Please take a few minutes to answer the following questions. To ensure complete confidentiality, your name and any identifying characteristics of the information you provide will be changed.

1. What specifically are you doing differently than you were before?
2. What results are you getting?
   How are your emotions being affected?
   How is your relationship being affected?
   How is your life experience being affected?
3. Which techniques are proving most helpful to you?
4. Which techniques are least helpful?
5. How have you adapted the techniques you are using to fit your particular needs?

We also welcome comments about this book.

A. What did you like most about it? Like least?
B. Which parts were the most helpful? Least helpful?
C. Which parts, if any, would you like to see clarified or simplified?
D. What information, if any, would you like to see added?

Thank you for your help. Send your response to

Dr. Albert Ellis & Marcia Grad Powers
Wilshire Book Company
9731 Variel Avenue
Chatsworth, California 91311-4315

Or e-mail us at mgpowers@mpowers.com

Suggested Reading

The following references include a number of Rational Emotive Behavior Therapy (REBT) and Cognitive Behavior Therapy publications which may be useful for self-help purposes. Many of these materials are obtainable from the Albert Ellis Institute, 45 East 65th Street, New York, N.Y. 10021-6593. The Institute's free catalog may be ordered on weekdays by phone (212-535-0822), by fax (212-249-3582) or e-mail (orders@rebt.org).

Alberti, R. & Emmons, R. (1995). *Your Perfect Right*. 7th ed. San Luis Obispo, CA: Impact. Original Ed., 1970.

Barlow, D. H., & Craske, N. G. (1994). *Mastery of Your Anxiety and Panic*. Albany, NY: Graywind Publications.

Beck, A. T. (1988). *Love is Not Enough*. New York: Harper & Row.

Burns, D. D. (1989). *Feeling Good Handbook*. New York: Morrow.Dryden, W. (1994). *Overcoming Guilt!* London: Sheldon.

Dryden, W., & Gordon, J. (1991). *Think Your Way to Happiness*. London: Sheldon Press.

Ellis, A. (1988). *How to Stubbornly Refuse to Make Yourself Miserable About Anything — Yes, Anything!* Secaucus, NJ: Lyle Stuart.

Ellis, A. (1998). *How to Control Your Anxiety Before It Controls You*. Secaucus, NJ: Carol Publishing Group.

Ellis, A. (1999). *How to Make Yourself Happy and Remarkably Less Disturbable*. San Luis Obispo, CA: Impact Publishers.

Ellis, A., & Becker, I. (1982). *A Guide to Personal Happiness*. North Hollywood, CA: Wilshire Book Company.

Ellis, A., & Harper, R. A. (1997). *A Guide to Rational Living*. North Hollywood, CA: Wilshire Book Company.

Ellis, A., & Knaus, W. (1977). *Overcoming Procrastination*. New York: New American Library.

Ellis, A., & Lange, A. (1994). *How to Keep People From Pushing Your Buttons*. New York: Carol Publishing Group.

Ellis, A., & Tafrate, R. C. (1997). *How to Control Your Anger Before It Controls You.*Secaucus, NJ: Birch Lane Press.

Ellis, A., & Velten, E. (1992). *When AA Doesn't Work for You: Rational Steps for Quitting Alcohol.* New York: Barricade Books.

Ellis, A., & Velten, E. (1998). *Optimal Aging: Get Over Getting Older.* Chicago: Open Court Publishing.

Fitzmaurice, K. E. (1997). *Attitude Is All You Need.* Omaha, NE: Palm Tree Publishers.Glasser, W. (1999). *Choice Theory.* New York: Harper Perennial.

Grad, M. (1986). *Charisma: How to get "that special magic."* North Hollywood, CA: Wilshire Book Company

Grad, M. (1995). *The Princess Who Believed in Fairy Tales.* North Hollywood, CA: Wilshire Book Company

Hauck, P. A. (1991). *Overcoming the Rating Game: Beyond Self-Love — Beyond Self-Esteem.* Louisville, KY: Westminster/John Knox.

Lazarus, A., & Lazarus, C. N. (1997). *The 60-Second Shrink.* San Luis Obispo: Impact.

Lazarus, A., Lazarus, C., & Fay, A. (1993). *Don't Believe It for a Minute: Forty Toxic Ideas That Are Driving You Crazy.* San Luis Obispo, CA: Impact Publishers.

Low, A. A. (1952). *Mental Health Through Will Training.* Boston: Christopher.

Miller, T. (1986). *The Unfair Advantage.* Manlius, NY: Horsesense, Inc.

Mills, D. (1993). *Overcoming Self-Esteem.* New York: Albert Ellis Institute.

Russell, B. (1950). *The Conquest of Happiness.* New York: New American Library.

Seligman, M. E. P. (1991). *Learned Optimism.* New York: Knopf.

Wolfe, J. L. (1992). *What to Do When He Has a Headache.* New York: Hyperion.

Young, H. S. (1974). *A Rational Counseling Primer.* New York: Institute For Rational-Emotive Therapy.

Index

Treat Yourself to This Fun, Inspirational Book and Discover How to
Find Happiness and Serenity . . . No Matter What Life Dishes Out

The Dragon Slayer
With a Heavy Heart

*This new book by bestselling author Marcia Powers promises to be
one of the most important you will ever read—and one of the most
entertaining, uplifting, and memorable.*

*It brings the Serenity Prayer—which for years has been the guiding
light of 12-step programs worldwide—to everyone . . . and teaches
both new and longtime devotees how to apply it most effectively to
their lives.*

Sometimes things happen we wish hadn't. Sometimes things *don't*
happen we wish *would*. In the course of living, problems arise, both
big and small. We might wish our past had been different or that *we*
could be different. We struggle through disappointments and
frustrations, losses and other painful experiences.

As hard as we may try to be strong, to have a good attitude, not to
let things get us down, we don't always succeed. We get upset. We
worry. We feel stressed. We get depressed. We get angry. We do the
best we can and wait for things to *get* better so we can *feel* better. In
the meantime, our hearts may grow heavy . . . perhaps very heavy.

That's what happened to Duke the Dragon Slayer. In fact, *his*
heart grew *so* heavy with all that was wrong, with all that was not the
way it should be, with all that was unfair, that he became desperate to
lighten it—and set forth on the Path of Serenity to find out how.

Accompany Duke on this life-changing adventure. His guides will
be your guides. His answers will be your answers. His tools will be
your tools. His success will be your success. And by the time he is
heading home, both Duke and you will know how to take life's inevitable lumps and bumps in stride—and find happiness and serenity
anytime . . . even when you really, REALLY wish some things were
different.

Available wherever books are sold or send $12.00 (CA res. $12.99) plus $2.00 S/H
to Wilshire Book Co., 9731 Variel Avenue, Chatsworth, CA 91311-4315.

For our complete catalog, visit our Web site at www.mpowers.com.

I invite you to meet an extraordinary princess and accompany her on an enlightening journey. You will laugh with her and cry with her, learn with her and grow with her . . . and she will become a dear friend you will never forget.

Marcia Grad Powers

1 MILLION COPIES SOLD WORLDWIDE

The Princess Who Believed in Fairy Tales

"Here is a very special book that will guide you lovingly into a new way of thinking about yourself and your life so that the future will be filled with hope and love and song."

OG MANDINO
Author, *The Greatest Salesman in the World*

The Princess Who Believed in Fairy Tales by Marcia Grad is a personal growth book of the rarest kind. It's a delightful, humor-filled story you will experience so deeply that it can literally change your feelings about yourself, your relationships, and your life.

The princess's journey of self-discovery on the Path of Truth is an eye-opening, inspiring, empowering psychological and spiritual journey that symbolizes the one we all take through life as we separate illusion from reality, come to terms with our childhood dreams and pain, and discover who we really are and how life works.

If you have struggled with childhood pain, with feelings of not being good enough, with the loss of your dreams, or if you have been disappointed in your relationships, this book will prove to you that happy endings—and new beginnings—are always possible. Or, if you simply wish to get closer to your own truth, the princess will guide you.

The universal appeal of this book has resulted in its translation into numerous languages.

Excerpts from Readers' Heartfelt Letters

"*The Princess* is truly a gem! Though I've read a zillion self-help and spiritual books, I got more out of this one than from any other one I've ever read. It is just too illuminating and full of wisdom to ever be able to thank you enough. The friends and family I've given copies to have raved about it."

"*The Princess* is powerful, insightful, and beautifully written. I am seventy years old and have seldom encountered greater wisdom. I've been waiting to read this book my entire life. You are a psychologist, a guru, a saint, and an angel all wrapped up into one. I thank you with all my heart."

Available wherever books are sold or send $12.00 (CA res. $12.99) plus $2.00 S/H to Wilshire Book Co., 9731 Variel Avenue, Chatsworth, California 91311-4315

For our complete catalog, visit our Web site at www.mpowers.com.

For every man who wants to shed his armor—and for the women who care about them...

KNIGHTS WITHOUT ARMOR

If you are struggling to rid yourself of heavy old restrictive armor that limits pleasure and joy in your life, hurts your relationships, damages your health, causes you to do destructive things to yourself and others—or if someone you care about is engaged in this struggle—*Knights Without Armor* is for you.

For centuries men have been taught from childhood that encasing themselves in armor is an integral part of being a man. And some men are further trapped by roles and jobs that demand they be tough and cold and hard as steel. They use psychological armor to forge ahead and to protect themselves from the potential ravages of what they confront day after day.

For many, maintaining their armor results in their walling themselves off from their feelings and from other people, which can come at a very high cost—isolation, confusion, frustration, anger, depression, addictions, troubled relationships, stress-related illnesses. But they fear that if they remove their armor, they may lose their strength, their power—even their masculinity.

Not so! says *Knights Without Armor*. Living the myth of the lone hero who conquers all through the force of his will is not the *only* way—or the *best* way—to be strong and powerful. This book is an adventure of self-discovery for male readers. The "Twelve Tasks of Men" guides them past the problems they have opening up their lives, and the "Male Manifesto" clarifies what it means to be a man. The adventure for women is in gaining insight into their man's quest to find a new way to live in the world.

For a beautiful, 294-page hardcover edition of *Knights Without Armor: A Practical Guide for Men in Quest of the Masculine Soul* by Aaron R. Kipnis, Ph.D.—psychotherapist, leader of men's groups, and expert in modern man's quest to live a new masculine role—order online at www.mpowers.com or send $10.00 (CA res. $10.83) plus $2.00 S/H to Wilshire Book Company, 9731 Variel Avenue, Chatsworth, CA 91311-4315.

An Unforgettable Treasure
Of Laughter and Wisdom

THE KNIGHT IN RUSTY ARMOR

2 MILLION COPIES SOLD WORLDWIDE

This story is guaranteed to captivate your imagination as it helps you discover the secret of what is most important in life. It's a delightful tale of a desperate knight in search of his true self.

The Knight in Rusty Armor by Robert Fisher is one of Wilshire Book Company's most popular titles. It's available in numerous languages and has become an international bestseller.

Join the knight as he faces a life-changing dilemma upon discovering that he is trapped in his armor, just as we may be trapped in *our* armor—an invisible one we put on to protect ourselves from others and from various aspects of life.

As the knight searches for a way to free himself, he receives guidance from the wise sage Merlin the Magician, who encourages him to embark on the most difficult crusade of his life. The knight takes up the challenge and travels the Path of Truth, where he meets his real self for the first time and confronts the Universal Truths that govern his life—and ours.

The knight's journey reflects our own, filled with hope and despair, belief and disillusionment, laughter and tears. His insights become our insights as we follow along on his intriguing adventure of self-discovery. Anyone who has ever struggled with the meaning of life and love will discover profound wisdom and truth as this unique fantasy unfolds.

The Knight in Rusty Armor will expand your mind, touch your heart, and nourish your soul.

THE KNIGHT IN RUSTY ARMOR MUSIC TAPE

Treat yourself to the soundtrack of the musical production of *The Knight in Rusty Armor*, narrated by Robert Fisher.

How You Can Have Confidence and Power in Dealing with People

A major key to success in your business and personal life is knowing how to deal with people. In fact, studies have shown that knowing how to deal with people is 85 to 90 percent of business and professional success, and 90 to 95 percent of personal happiness.

Now here's some great news. Dealing effectively with people is a skill you can learn, just as you learned to ride a bicycle, drive an automobile, or play the piano.

Discover how you can get what you want and be the way you want to be by tapping into your hidden assets. Assets you may not even realize you have. Assets that can transform an ordinary person into an extraordinary one. Assets that can give you more confidence and personal power than you ever thought possible.

Find out how to

- Feel confident in any business or social situation
- Win others to your way of thinking
- Understand and get along with people
- Make it easy for people to like you
- Create a positive and lasting impression
- Help others feel comfortable and friendly — instantly
- Make new friends and keep them
- Find love and build relationships that work

The way you lived yesterday determined your today. But the way you live today will determine your tomorrow. Every day is a new opportunity to become the way you want to be and to have your life become what you want it to be.

Take the first step toward becoming all you're capable of being. Read Marcia Grad's book *Charisma*, which teaches a proven step-by-step plan to help anyone develop the ultimate in personal power. Then get ready for an incredible adventure that will change you and your life forever.

WILSHIRE SELF-IMPROVEMENT LIBRARY

RECOVERY

____DRAGON SLAYER WITH A HEAVY HEART Marcia Powers 12.00
____KNIGHT IN RUSTY ARMOR Robert Fisher 7.00
____KNIGHTS WITHOUT ARMOR (Hardcover) Aaron R. Kipnis, Ph.D. 10.00
____PRINCESS WHO BELIEVED IN FAIRY TALES Marcia Grad 12.00
____SECRET OF OVERCOMING VERBAL ABUSE Dr. Albert Ellis & Marcia Grad Powers . 12.00

SELF-HELP & INSPIRATIONAL

____CHANGE YOUR VOICE, CHANGE YOUR LIFE Morton Cooper, Ph.D. 10.00
____CHARISMA—HOW TO GET "THAT SPECIAL MAGIC" Marcia Grad 10.00
____DAILY POWER FOR JOYFUL LIVING Dr. Donald Curtis 7.00
____DRAGON SLAYER WITH A HEAVY HEART Marcia Powers 12.00
____DYNAMIC THINKING Melvin Powers 7.00
____GREATEST POWER IN THE UNIVERSE U.S. Andersen 10.00
____GROW RICH WHILE YOU SLEEP Ben Sweetland 10.00
____GROW RICH WITH YOUR MILLION DOLLAR MIND Brian Adams 10.00
____GROWTH THROUGH REASON Albert Ellis, Ph.D. 10.00
____GUIDE TO PERSONAL HAPPINESS Albert Ellis, Ph.D. & Irving Becker, Ed.D. 10.00
____GUIDE TO RATIONAL LIVING Albert Ellis, Ph.D. & R. Harper, Ph.D. 15.00
____HANDWRITING ANALYSIS MADE EASY John Marley 10.00
____HANDWRITING TELLS Nadya Olyanova 10.00
____HOW TO ATTRACT GOOD LUCK A.H.Z. Carr 10.00
____HOW TO DEVELOP A WINNING PERSONALITY Martin Panzer 10.00
____HOW TO DEVELOP AN EXCEPTIONAL MEMORY Young & Gibson 10.00
____HOW TO LIVE WITH A NEUROTIC Albert Ellis, Ph.D. 10.00
____HOW TO SUCCEED Brian Adams 10.00
____I CAN Ben Sweetland..10.00
____I WILL Ben Sweetland 10.00
____KNIGHT IN RUSTY ARMOR Robert Fisher 7.00
____LAW OF SUCCESS IN SIXTEEN LESSONS Napoleon Hill (Two-Volume Set) 30.00
____MAGIC IN YOUR MIND U.S. Andersen 15.00
____MAGIC OF THINKING SUCCESS Dr. David J. Schwartz 10.00
____MAGIC POWER OF YOUR MIND Walter M. Germain 10.00
____NEVER UNDERESTIMATE THE SELLING POWER OF A WOMAN Dottie Walters ... 7.00
____PRINCESS WHO BELIEVED IN FAIRY TALES Marcia Grad 12.00
____PSYCHO-CYBERNETICS Maxwell Maltz, M.D. 10.00
____PSYCHOLOGY OF HANDWRITING Nadya Olyanova 10.00
____SALES CYBERNETICS Brian Adams 10.00
____SECRET OF OVERCOMING VERBAL ABUSE Dr. Albert Ellis & Marcia Grad Powers . 12.00
____SECRET OF SECRETS U.S. Andersen 10.00
____SELF-THERAPY FOR THE STUTTERER Malcolm Frazer 10.00
____STOP COMMITTING VOICE SUICIDE Morton Cooper, Ph.D....................10.00
____SUCCESS CYBERNETICS U.S. Andersen 10.00
____10 DAYS TO A GREAT NEW LIFE William E. Edwards 3.00
____THINK AND GROW RICH Napoleon Hill 12.00
____THINK LIKE A WINNER Walter Doyle Staples, Ph.D. 15.00
____THREE MAGIC WORDS U.S. Andersen 15.00
____TREASURY OF COMFORT Edited by Rabbi Sidney Greenberg 15.00
____TREASURY OF THE ART OF LIVING Edited by Rabbi Sidney Greenberg 10.00
____WHAT YOUR HANDWRITING REVEALS Albert E. Hughes 4.00
____WINNING WITH YOUR VOICE Morton Cooper, Ph.D. 10.00
____YOUR SUBCONSCIOUS POWER Charles M. Simmons 7.00

Available wherever books are sold or from the publisher.
Please add $2.00 S/H for each book ordered.

Wilshire Book Company
9731 Variel Avenue, Chatsworth, California 91311-4315
For our complete catalog, visit our Web site at www.mpowers.com.

Books by Melvin Powers

HOW TO GET RICH IN MAIL ORDER

1. How to Develop Your Mail Order Expertise 2. How to Find a Unique Product or Service to Sell 3. How to Make Money with Classified Ads 4. How to Make Money with Display Ads 5. The Unlimited Potential for Making Money with Direct Mail 6. How to Copycat Successful Mail Order Operations 7. How I Created a Bestseller Using the Copycat Technique 8. How to Start and Run a Profitable Mail Order Special Interest Book Business 9. I Enjoy Selling Books by Mail—Some of My Successful Ads 10. Five of My Most Successful Direct Mail Pieces That Sold and Are Selling Millions of Dollars' Worth of Books 11. Melvin Powers's Mail Order Success Strategy—Follow it and You'll Become a Millionaire 12. How to Sell Your Products to Mail Order Companies, Retail Outlets, Jobbers, and Fund Raisers for Maximum Distribution and Profit 13. How to Get Free Display Ads and Publicity that Will Put You on the Road to Riches 14. How to Make Your Advertising Copy Sizzle 15. Questions and Answers to Help You Get Started Making Money 16. A Personal Word from Melvin Powers 17. How to Get Started 18. Selling Products on Television   8½" x 11½" — 352 Pages . . . $20.00

MAKING MONEY WITH CLASSIFIED ADS

1. Getting Started with Classified Ads 2. Everyone Loves to Read Classified Ads 3. How to Find a Money-Making Product 4. How to Write Classified Ads that Make Money 5. What I've Learned from Running Thousands of Classified Ads 6. Classified Ads Can Help You Make Big Money in Multi-Level Programs 7. Two-Step Classified Ads Made Me a Multi-Millionaire—They Can Do the Same for You! 8. One-Inch Display Ads Can Work Wonders 9. Display Ads Can Make You a Fortune Overnight 10. Although I Live in California, I Buy My Grapefruit from Florida 11. Nuts and Bolts of Mail Order Success 12. What if You Can't Get Your Business Running Successfully? What's Wrong? How to Correct it 13. Strategy for Mail Order Success   8½" x 11½" — 240 Pages . . . $20.00

HOW TO SELF-PUBLISH YOUR BOOK AND HAVE THE FUN AND EXCITEMENT OF BEING A BEST-SELLING AUTHOR

1. Who is Melvin Powers? 2. What is the Motivation Behind Your Decision to Publish Your Book? 3. Why You Should Read This Chapter Even if You Already Have an Idea for a Book 4. How to Test the Salability of Your Book Before You Write One Word 5. How I Achieved Sales Totaling $2,000,000 on My Book *How to Get Rich in Mail Order* 6. How to Develop a Second Career by Using Your Expertise 7. How to Choose an Enticing Book Title 8. Marketing Strategy 9. Success Stories 10. How to Copyright Your Book 11. How to Write a Winning Advertisement 12. Advertising that Money Can't Buy 13. Questions and Answers to Help You Get Started 14. Self-Publishing and the Midas Touch
8½" x 11½" — 240 Pages . . . $20.00

A PRACTICAL GUIDE TO SELF-HYPNOSIS

1. What You Should Know about Self-Hypnosis 2. What about the Dangers of Hypnosis? 3. Is Hypnosis the Answer? 4. How Does Self-Hypnosis Work? 5. How to Arouse Yourself From the Self-Hypnotic State 6. How to Attain Self-Hypnosis 7. Deepening the Self-Hypnotic State 8. What You Should Know about Becoming an Excellent Subject 9. Techniques for Reaching the Somnambulistic State 10. A New Approach to Self-Hypnosis 11. Psychological Aids and Their Function 12. Practical Applications of Self-Hypnosis
144 Pages . . . $10.00

Available at your bookstore or directly from Wilshire Book Company.
Please add $2.00 shipping and handling for each book ordered.

Wilshire Book Company
9731 Variel Avenue, Chatsworth, California 91311-4315

For our complete catalog, visit our Web site at www.mpowers.com.